Rifles, Rangers & Revolution

A study of the fantastic arms of 1776 including the P1776 Ferguson Breechloader & the P1776 muzzleloading rifles, the Brown Bess musket, the Eliott Light Dragoon pistol, the Potter Saber and the little Grasshopper Cannon.

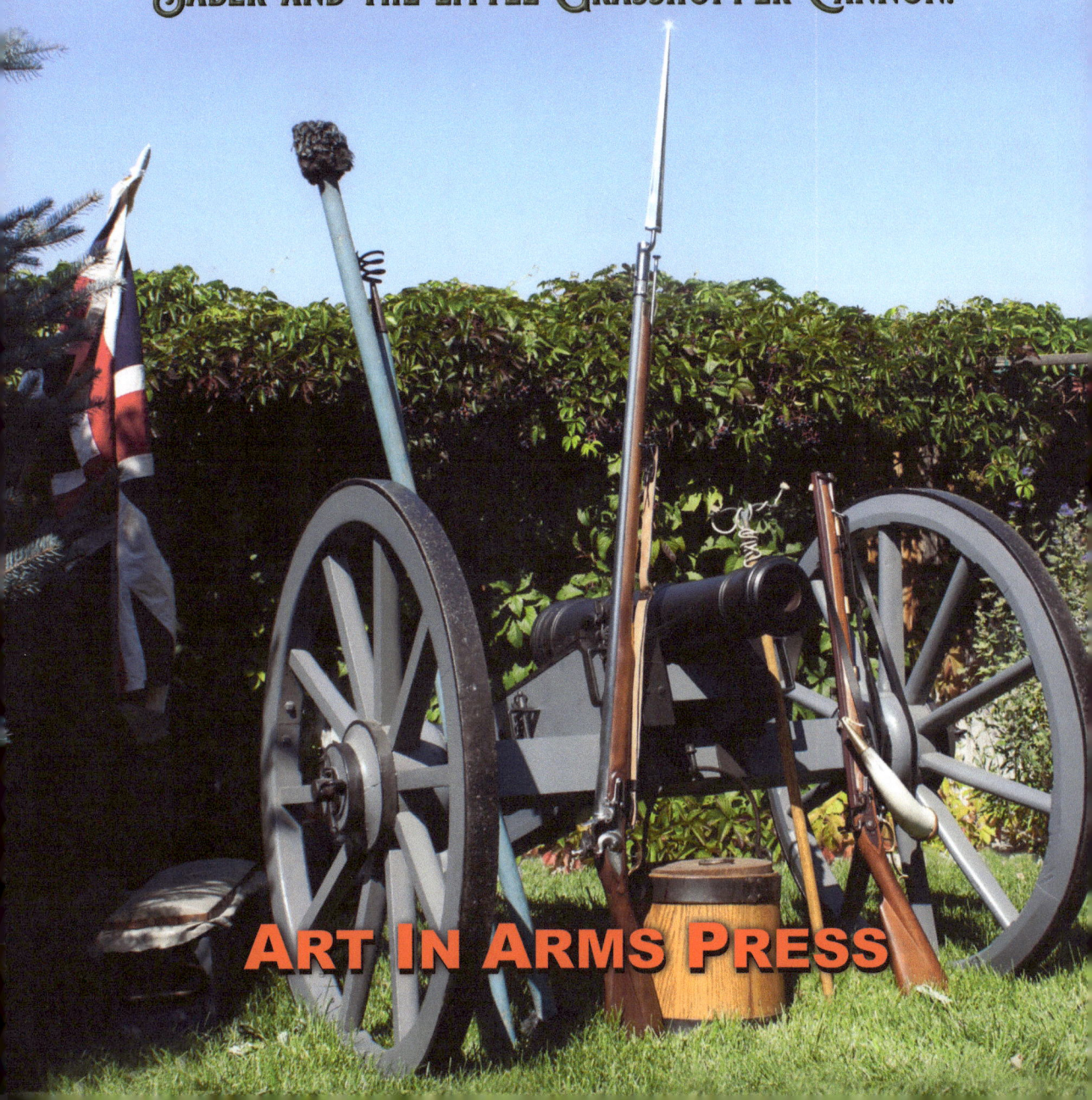

Art In Arms Press

The Art in Arms Press Book No. 3

Visit the Art In Arms Website!
www.ArtInArmsPress.com

Art In Arms Press
9732 Pyramid Hwy #113, Sparks, NV 89441, USA
email: info@ArtInArmsPress.com
Attention: Jeff John, Publisher

Rifles, Rangers & Revolution

By Jeff John

©2020 Art In Arms Press
ISBN: 978-1-7326395-6-0
1st Print Edition

Executive Editor: Payton Miller

All rights reserved. No part of this publication may be reproduced, retransmitted or copied by any method without the author's consent, except for brief quotes as part of a review.

Built with Affinity software. Photos taken with Canon cameras and lenses.

Acknowledgement

I GREW UP hearing tales of the hapless Redcoats armed with hopelessly inaccurate muskets wilting under the dauntless onslaught of Colonial riflemen, as well as stories of the British forgetting everything about rifles upon losing the colonies. Such stories eventually brought out the contrarian in me. It seemed some puzzle pieces were missing, especially since the British army had already fought a war on this continent and were very familiar with the locals, indigenous populations, and the use of rifles. It lead me on a journey to see whether these stories were fact, fiction or something in between.

As the rifle myth quickly unravelled, it was obvious there was a deeper story. Two meticulous books by DeWitt Bailey on British arms used in the Americas proved an invaluable aid in understanding much of the nuts and bolts of the guns and gear used during the period from the French & Indian War through the Napoleonic Wars.

Bailey's books led me to building a Revolutionary War-era British rifle—the Pattern 1776. The search for units using them led me to the Queen's Rangers, an intrepid group of American Loyalists fielding most of the technological wonder weapons of 1776 as it turned out. The Queen's Rangers in turn offered a glimpse into all the strange technology the cauldron of war created. The Rangers used it all, and the unit was fairly well documented since their commander left behind a Journal of Operations.

Studying the Rangers led to Patrick Ferguson and his breechloading rifle. Ferguson served with the Rangers initially. All the stories I'd read about him also seemed half-baked and resembled the Redcoat vs. Rifleman stories. To me, the banter for and against was not grounded in fact, but in imagination. By learning to shoot the reproduction Ferguson rifle, its promise was proved (at least to me), thanks to Ricky Roberts and Bryan Brown. They are two living historians whose book *Every Insult & Indignity* smoked out how the Ferguson worked best. Following their methods—based on a study of Ferguson's actual writings—I was able to shoot the Ferguson rifle like the wonder weapon it was originally presented as being, and discovered its faults.

The guns and gear represented here are all reproductions. You need few fingers to count the number of surviving rifles. Even muskets, sabers and pistols are quite scarce and all are top-tier collectibles. Leather gear and uniforms are almost all gone, and were reconstructed using original paintings, the Ranger's Journal, Ferguson's letters and advice from many reenactors and sutlers. Much of the gear is based on speculation, however, since the original sources aren't often particularly descriptive I've tried to make the gear as accurate as possible, but take it with a grain of salt. Don't be surprised if my concepts don't agree with other researchers.

Artist Don Troiani is a master of these subjects and has an intuitive sense for what these men might have worn based on his vast knowledge and a personal collection of original items. His paintings helped fill in the gaps.

Thanks to the Toronto Public Library for access to original art done in the time by Ranger Capt. Murray, and for Simcoe's portrait. Studying Murray's paintings helped with the gear as worn by the Rangers.

Special thanks to Jess Melot of The Rifle Shoppe, who made the kits for both P1776 breech and muzzleloading rifles from the only known complete examples. Without those meticulous reproductions, all this would be in vain. Discussions of shooting theory with Jess led to a better understanding of the way things were, including the special principals of materials such as wrought iron, which we no longer use in gun building, but can't replicate with modern steels. The brown finish on these rifles, something much debated, is based on conversations with Jess, who disassembled the rifles to create the molds and discovered their original brown finish in protected areas. His observations were instrumental in understanding their construction, too.

Special thanks to the Queen's York Rangers, who graciously allowed me to send photographer Anne De Hass into their Officer's Mess in Toronto, Canada, where the original colours are on display. To my knowledge, this is the first time they will be presented to the public at large since their last furling at Yorktown on October 19, 1781 (unless you are a frequent visitor to the Art In Arms Press website, that is).

Finally, at the end of it all is strange story connecting the manufacture of cannon to the Industrial Revolution, something most histories treat as two independent events. This journey goes back 100 years farther and contests some established history (it's the beginning of another line of research). Thanks to the Royal Artillery Museum for the tips on books, and especially member Rick Hatton who helped me with the construction of artillery ammunition, and a big thanks to the descendants of Jan Verbruggen for graciously allowing the use of some of the Jan Verbruggen's original Foundry drawings of Woolwich Arsenal painted in the 1770s to illustrate the chapters on cannon!

These little books are meant to cover topics usually reserved for much larger (and expensive) hardcover books. This topic grew far past the first two, but there was that much to learn! I hope you enjoy it. If you have a question or comment, please contact me. An email address is provided on the title pages. Thanks for reading!—*Jeff John*

Table of Contents

Chapter 1: An Explosion of Innovative Technology — 9
   New rifles, new cannon and new tactics.

Chapter 2: A Legendary Leader — 13
   The Rangers rise again.

Chapter 3: A Coveted Command — 15
   Leading from the front.

Chapter 4: Hearts & Minds — 19
   The civilian equation.

Chapter 5: A Green Revolution — 21
   Not "uniformly red" as the opposition discovered.

Part II: Small Arms of the Rangers

Chapter 6: The Platypus Rifle — 23
   The unique muzzleloading P1776 rifle shared features with a musket.

Chapter 7: Rifle Ammunition — 29
   An improved spin on versatility.

Chapter 8: Handling & Tactics — 33
   Employment of the P1776.

Chapter 9: Traveling Light — 35
   Always prepared for action.

Notes on Cleaning: Oh! What an odious chore! — 38
   However necessary, it wasn't easy or fun.

Chapter 10: The Ferguson Rifle — 41
   A truly "revolutionary" concept!

Chapter 11: The Paoli Massacre — 51
   A squad of Ferguson's Rifles springs a bloody surprise.

Chapter 12: What Became of the Fergusons? — 53
   The rifles and the men vanish from memory.

Chapter 13: Ferguson's Promise Lost — 57
   "What Might Have Been…"

Chapter 14: The Brown Bess — 61
   Anchor of the Thin Red Line.

Chapter 15: Cavalry — 67
   Projecting Force by Horse.

Chapter 16: Arms of the Cavalry — 73
   Sabres, rifles, carbines, pistols.

Chapter 17: The Chicanery Of Action   75
    Always Practice to Deceive.
Chapter 18: Spencer's Ordinary   77
    The Master of Chicanery at work again!
Part III
Chapter 19: The Grasshopper Gun   83
    A purpose-built cannon for America.
Chapter 20: A Modern Era   85
    Let the Industrial Revolution begin!
Chapter 21: Three 3-pounders   89
    There was surprising variety in the little guns.
Chapter 22: Puzzles & Power   91
    Small gun, small punch.
Chapter 23: Pounds & Power   92
    Less can be more.
Chapter 24: Bait & Switch   95
    The Osborne's.
Chapter 26: One Effective Insect   99
    The Grasshopper re-imagined.
Chapter 27: The Price of Poundage   102
    Moving iron is hard work!
Chapter 28: Manning a Gun   105
    A glimpse at the tools of the trade.
Chapter 29: Yorktown   109
    The beginning of the end of British rule.
Part IV: Repros at the Range
Chapter 30: The Ferguson   113
    Easy to shoot, accurate to boot!
Chapter 31: Shooting The Pattern 1776   118
    A (not so) "common" muzzleloading rifle.
Chapter 32: The Brown Bess   121
    Repro quality levels.
Chapter 33: The Eliott Light Dragoon Pistol   125
    The Loyalist Arms import cleaned up nicely and shoots well.
Appendix i: Footnotes & Further Reading   128
Appendix ii: Notes About the Paintings   130
Appendix iii: Weights and Measures of the Arms   131
Appendix iv: Another Revolution Started with a Bang!   137
Appendix v: Sutlers Row & About the Author   146

Rifles, Rangers & Revolution

Part 1
Chapter 1
An Explosion of Innovative Technology
New rifles, new cannon and new tactics.

ENGLAND FIELDED THREE state-of-the-art weapons in 1776 to quell the Revolution in the Colonies. All were groundbreaking in one way or another. The one with the longest lasting effect was a cannon made using the most modern of foundry techniques. The new system turned out superior cannon tubes far faster than ever before. The technological breakthrough led to the steam engine and the Industrial Revolution.

Next was a common rifle, but unique in being designed for quick loading and being used by both cavalry and infantry, thus filling the gap left when American riflemen chose to fight for independence. Lastly was a revolutionary breechloading rifle that could have revolutionized warfare, but whose promise was lost when its inventor was wounded, then killed.

Fortunately for the United States, the outcome wasn't decided by technology. It's still amazing to find the 13 Colonies won, survived the formation of a republic, and endured. It was one of histories few revolutions not devolving into mass murder and despotism. God Bless America!

Throughout the Revolution, the normally hidebound British army allowed generous rein to young commanders such as Lt. Col. John Graves Simcoe of the Queen's Rangers. He and like-minded men, including Hessian Capt. Johann von Ewald, helped lay the foundation of change England would draw on to create their soon-to-be-dominant professional army, just in time for the next "world war."

The tactics and techniques developed in concert with the Hessian rifleman paved the road for Britain's rethinking of its military doctrine in time to stop

The screw-breech Ferguson rifle (left) and the tactical doctrine devised by Patrick Ferguson were truly revolutionary. His severe wound, the dissolution of his company then his death forever capped its promise. The Ferguson rifle weighed as much as the musket, delivered accurate fire at three times the musket's range, was faster to load, used simpler ammunition and mounted a bayonet. An unproven wartime product, its defects only needed the refinement all weapons systems undergo before achieving acceptable perfection.

the world's next truly relentless menace in one Napoleon Bonaparte.

The Queen's Rangers were a small, complete regiment fielding infantry, cavalry and artillery to deliver and defend against acts of "little war" (what we now call "guerrilla warfare"), something at which Indians and Americans excelled. As defined by the Marechal de Saxe prior to the Seven Year's War (French & Indian War here), it consists of war "waged by small detachments, consisting in patrols, raids, the gathering of information, ambushes, reconnaissance, protection of the main army from surprise attacks, foraging,

Lt. Col. John Graves Simcoe by Jean Laurent Mosnier (1791). Print courtesy the Toronto Public Library.

capturing of prisoners." (14) The Queen's Loyal American Rangers were equally at home delivering all aspects of "little war," and capably accomplished the tasks outlined by de Saxe.

Others in Europe maintained units honed to perfection in these tactics, including the Austrian Grenz Corps which ably guarded the Austro/Hungarian Empire's frontier against constant incursions of Ottoman raiders. Grenz were issued a unique over/under, rifle/smoothbore Doppelstütz, giving them the unique tactical advantage of both precision and volume fire.

While issue of a purpose-designed rifle hadn't really entered British military thinking as a necessary, regular component of the army, they had issued rifles to the "best marksmen" on a small scale with rifles purchased on the open market since the 1740s. Some had bayonets, but the practice wouldn't catch on (for awhile at least). In Europe, rifle use had been standard doctrine in many German Landgraves, or States, since the 1740s as well. Rifle-armed Jäger units (jäger means "hunter" in German) were recruited from men experienced in stalking and woodcraft. These units served well during the Seven Years' War, and most German states maintained seed units after the end of hostilities to keep the concept alive.

Having lost the use of American riflemen at the beginning of the Revolution, England used a two-prong solution. The first was to immediately rent companies of German Jägers (the state of Hesse-Kassel sent the most, giving rise to calling all German troops "Hessians"). The second was to arm select English and Scottish soldiers with a German-inspired rifle, the majority of which were built in Birmingham, England.

The rifle with its fussy manual of arms remained sidelined by generals on both sides mainly concerned with forming on the battlefield in lines and columns opposite each other, and then slugging it out toe-to-toe with artillery, cavalry charges, musketry, then bayonets until one side broke.

Where the rifle shined was in fighting the little war. During an army's movements, rifle-armed troops kept the enemy farther at bay as the rest of the army marched toward its business or left behind their last bit of work. But even among the light infantry—including the Rangers—the rifle was a specialty weapon. The bread-and-butter tool, the one by which all battles were settled, remained the smoothbore musket with its simpler manual of arms fixed with a bayonet (and would for more than another half century).

Most Light Infantry units were a single company within a regiment. The Queen's Loyal American Rangers were unique in that they were a complete, if small, regiment. They were commanded by Lt. Col. John Graves Simcoe from 1777 to 1781, but he wasn't the original commander.

Chapter 2
A Legendary Leader
The Rangers rise again.

ONE OF THE FINEST companies of Light Infantry was Rogers' Rangers led by Major Robert Rogers during the French & Indian War. Rogers, a legend in his own time, returned to America in 1776 to found the Queen's Loyal American Rangers initially raised from loyalist colonials. The fact the Queen's Rangers are little known in the United States is mostly because they were on the other side. But Robert Rogers was—and still is—a well-known name in American history.

The legacy of Rogers' Rangers during the 1750s has shined for more than 270 years. Rogers' Standing Orders to his men still ring true today, and have been modernized and codified by the U.S. Army for today's Rangers. He didn't become a hero the second time around, and even England has largely forgotten him as well as his contributions.

While some of Rogers' original Rangers rose to prominence during the American Revolution fighting for independence, Rogers' personal motives for returning to an America in conflict remain unclear. Rogers claimed his goal was to look for the fabled Northwest Passage, and that he came here with backing for the project from England. It was a thin story.

He arrived from England in 1775 still on half-pay as a former British officer, was met with suspicion, and his services turned down by George Washington. Because it was feared he was a spy, Rogers was kept under close watch by the Continentals, but slipped away. He offered his services to General Sir William Howe, raising the Queen's Loyal American Rangers in 1776 with loyalist colonials and some of his former Rangers. The regiment was named in honor King George's wife Charlotte, and became the "1st American Regiment," a name still in use to this day.

The Colours of the Queen's Rangers (left) are the oldest known military colours in North America, and were taken back to England by Lt. Col. Simcoe after the Battle of Yorktown in 1781. They came home to Canada in 1920s and, much later, were painstakingly restored by the Royal Ontario Museum. They now hang in the Officer's Mess of the Queen's York Rangers based in Toronto, Canada. They are not on public display and no picture of them existed until Art In Arms Press commissioned photographer Anne de Haas to take these (see Chapter 29 for more).

The Queen's Rangers had a rocky start. It was well accepted a "light corps" was composed of unusually rough characters, but the composition of the officers chosen by Roberts' left his fellow British officers aghast. Rogers quickly proved his worth by being instrumental in the capture and hanging of Continental spy Nathan Hale. Hale was engaged in a tavern by the hard-drinking Rogers, who coaxed him into speaking just a bit too freely.

But drink also led to Rogers' downfall. Lt. Col. Robert Rogers was replaced in January 1777— along with most of his officers—after being surprised by a Colonial force as they lay asleep. Though the Rangers acquitted themselves well, what little respect Rogers and his Rangers had among his fellow officers disappeared, and Howe felt compelled to replace him. Because of his loyalist sympathies, the Massachusetts-born Rogers would be divorced by his wife and shunned by his former countrymen. He returned to England for his own safety and faded into obscurity, dying in 1795. Even the location of his grave has been forgotten.

Maj. Christopher French then commanded the Rangers for a short time until requesting he be returned to his original unit. He was replaced by Maj. James Wemyss of the 40th Regiment who commanded them from May 4 to October 14, 1777. Wemyss trained the Rangers vigorously, forming them into a disciplined unit. Under Wemyss the Rangers would acquit themselves well at the Battle of Brandywine in an action where Capt. Patrick Ferguson and his breechloading rifle (see Chapter 10) fought their single battle under Wemyss. Ferguson's wound at Brandywine ended that experiment.

Commendable Action

Two days after reviewing Gen. Kniphausen's account of Brandywine, Gen. Howe wrote, "The Commander in Chief desires to convey to the officers and men of the Queen's Rangers his approbation and acknowledgment for their spirited and gallant behavior in the engagement of the 11th instant, and to ensure them how well he is satisfied with their distinguished conduct on that day. His excellency only regrets their having suffered so much in the gallant execution of their duty." [1]

Wemyss was himself wounded at the Battle of Germantown just a short time after and, on October 15, 1777, Howe replaced him with Capt. John Graves Simcoe of the 40th Grenadiers. Simcoe then commanded the newly renamed Queen's Rangers (they dropped "Loyal American" from their official name) until the surrender at Yorktown. Wemyss transferred to the 63rd after recovering from his wounds, and would prove as big a terror in North Carolina fighting against Francis Marion—the "Swamp Fox" himself—as he was with the Rangers.

Chapter 3
A Coveted Command
Leading from the front.

COMMAND OF THE RANGERS was a post sought after by Simcoe, who later wrote, "The command of a light corps, or, as it is termed, the service of a partisan*, is generally esteemed the best mode of instruction for those who aim at higher stations; as it gives an opportunity of exemplifying professional acquisitions, fixes the habit of self-dependence for resources, and obliges duty subordinate officers can seldom exhibit, yet without which none can be qualified for any trust of importance." [1] Thus spoke the son of a late Captain in the Royal Navy (HMS Pembroke). Command of a light corps was the Army version of being captain of a frigate, a ship often operating independently with much freedom of action. On land, the independent command of a light corps routinely gave subordinate officers the opportunity to act as a general would, just on a smaller scale.

Although rarely ever at full strength after their formation, the Queen's Rangers were a complete regiment reinforced with detachments of the necessary types of soldiers for a given mission. A complete regiment, the Rangers fielded line infantry, grenadiers, riflemen including Hessian Jägers, Highlanders (the Scots were naturals as Light Infantry, and one of the first units to ask for rifles). Cavalry was soon added, composed of a scant dozen "Huzzars" in the beginning, and growing to between 30 and 100 on average including Dragoons, Mounted Rifles, and the occasional detached company as needed.

The Rangers drew artillery when necessary in the form of 3-pounder "Grasshoppers" and/or a 1½-pounder Amusette, along with a crew of Royal Artillery to serve them. Originally raised entirely of Americans, by the end of the war, only about 25 percent of the Rangers were Americans, and the rest recruited from other units, including men from Britain, Ireland, Scotland and a few Germans for good measure.

A Checkered Past

Historically, Light Infantry were generally reviled, especially in Europe. Led by rogue noblemen or elected officers, they were usually not subject to the fierce discipline and rote training most regular armies imposed. Their ranks could include thieves, cutthroats and other villains, and they were unwelcome

except in battle, where (for the most part) they proved valuable. Off the battlefield, they were known to commit crimes for which regular soldiers would be hanged or flogged and the officers cashiered.

The British reaction to Rogers' choice of officers is typical of the reaction to a light corps' staff and troops, but such criticism ended with his replacement. Howe was astute in giving the command to Simcoe, a man who understood the type of men he was commanding, and one endeavoring to bring out their best without resorting to the brutish treatment usually visited on wayward regulars. Simcoe set a tone in his training that made the Rangers a feared and dominant force. "To attain this employment was therefore an early object with the author [Simcoe]; nor could he be diverted from his purpose by the shameful character of dishonesty, rapine, and falsehood; supposed to attend it; at least by those who formed their judgment on the conversation of such officers as had been witness to the campaigns in Germany." [1]

Capt. Johann von Ewald of the Hesse-Kassel Jägers was witness to such depredations in Europe during the Seven Years' War. He served under Simcoe on many operations and wrote *Treatise on Partisan Warfare** after the Revolution noting the importance of such discipline, "Above all one can not deal harshly enough with those villains who mercilessly torment the peasants who are innocent of the war. The best thing to do is to chase such rabble away, since those who once stooped to plundering can never be trusted again, and they spoil the good soldiers as well." [14] Under Simcoe, such behavior would be firmly suppressed.

**The definition of Partisan in this case means troops raised outside of the regular army as were the Rangers from the loyal colonials. At the end of hostilities, partisan troops were released to return to their homes, and officers, who were promoted one rank upon volunteering, were returned to their original units and rank upon discharge.*

Most of this work is based on Lt. Col. John Graves Simcoe's *History of the Operations,* a journal kept during the war. It was fun to imagine him sitting at a portable desk writing his journal, general orders and other communiques sometimes by candlelight (here beeswax candles in "Brighton Buns" candle holders. Hussars (or Huzzars as Simcoe wrote) became a quick strike force and the means of rapid communication. They wore a tall shako with the Ranger's crescent moon symbol representing Diana, Goddess of the Hunt. Huzzars were lightly armed with Potter sword (bottom) and a pistol (such as an Eliott Light Dragoon pistol, above).

The smoothbore musket and bayonet was the staple of 18th century combat, and the Brown Bess was England's choice for more than 100 years. Simcoe had "Queen's Rangers" engraved atop the barrels. Green jackets instead of red, and black crossbelts were issued instead of white.

Chapter 4
Hearts & Minds
The civilian equation.

THE BRITISH WERE a little more sensitive in dealing with a civilian populace than is often popularly portrayed, at least in theory, and these theories dated back to experiences in the English Civil War between King Charles and the Parliament. They understood the majority of Americans were loyal subjects of the Crown, yet many could be easily turned to the rebel cause by ill treatment. Simcoe relates, "There is not an officer in the world who is ignorant, that permitting the soldier to plunder, or maraud, must inevitably destroy him; that, in a civil war, it must alienate the large body of the people who, in such a contest, are desirous of neutrality, and sour their minds into dissatisfaction: but, however obvious the necessity may be, there is nothing more difficult than for a commander in chief to prevent marauding…." Simcoe took care to keep temptation away from his men, "…he never halted, if he could avoid it, but in a wood; sent safeguards to every house; allowed no man, in marching, to quit his ranks…." [1]

Ewald adds, "Do not believe that you can gain the love of a soldier through an unpermissible kindness and indulgence at the expense of the poor peasant and by a policy contrary to all human nature. The soldier will try everything, if he gets away with it; all irregularities will eventually increase so much that they can not be corrected any more." [14]

The training Simcoe gave his Rangers differed from the rote drill of the regulars, too. Simcoe notes, "A light corps… employed on the duties of an outpost, has no opportunity of being instructed in the general discipline of the army, nor indeed was it very necessary: the most important duties, those of vigilance, activity, and patience of fatigue, were best learnt in the field; they were carefully instructed in those of firing, but above all, attention was paid to inculcate the use of the bayonet, and a total reliance on that weapon." Simcoe adds, "It was observed, that regularity in messing, and cleanliness in every respect, conduced to the health of the soldier…" [1]

It wasn't long before this philosophy was tested. During the winter of 1777, the Queen's Rangers kept open the roads from New York to Philadelphia, where the British were wintering, while Washington's army suffered at Valley Forge. Troops far from an army's discipline historically devolved to plundering the countryside, since they were out operating alone and in small groups, but not the Queen's Rangers. "[Simcoe] was, in general, successful in instilling into the minds of the men, that while they protected the country, the inhabitants would give every information of the enemy's movements and ambuscades.... On the contrary, the rebel patroles, who came to stop the markets, were considered by the country people as robbers.... The market people, who overnight would get into the woods, came out on the appearance of the corps, and proceeded uninterruptedly, and from market they had an escort...." [1]

Simcoe's teachings didn't always pay off. Later in the war, he arrived at headquarters only to find two of his Rangers accused of robbery and rape. An enquiry proved the robbery without doubt, and Lord Cornwallis ordered the men executed the next day.

This work in the winter of 1777 while the regular army rested, entailed long marches in inclement weather, sometimes severe, of up to 90 miles a week for the infantry and more for the flank companies, Highlanders and cavalry.

"The general mode that Major Simcoe adopted was, to keep perfectly secret the hour, the road, and the manner of his march; to penetrate, in one body, about ten miles in the country. This body generally marched in three divisions, one hundred yards from each other, so that it would have required a large force to have embraced the whole in ambuscade... [At] ten or twelve miles the corps divided, and ambuscaded different roads; and at the appointed time returned home. There was not a bye path or ford unknown, and the Huzzars would generally patrole some miles in front of the infantry.

The army regulars, hunkered in winter quarters, assumed these cold weather tasks assigned the Rangers would debilitate the corps and leave them unable to continue after the winter. On the contrary, "[By] these patroles, the corps was formed to that tolerance of fatigue and marching, which excelled that of the chosen light troops of the army...." [1] The endurance learned on this duty would serve the Rangers well in campaigns to come.

Chapter 5
A Green Revolution
Not "uniformly red" as the opposition discovered.

THE RANGERS KEPT their traditional green uniforms first seen in the French & Indian War throughout the conflict, even as the rest of the British Army switched to red. For the infantry, over the green coat went black accoutrements topped by a tall, black, mitre-style hat with a green and white plume at the side and a crescent moon in the front. The moon was inspired by the hunter's moon, a favorite of Diana, Roman Goddess of the Hunt. Long white breeches were worn and buckled over the shoes. Riflemen wore a short-tailed jacket and often moved with just rifle, horn and haversack or pouch.

It might seem strange to think of green as helping blend into the surroundings only to wear "white" trousers, but in those days, whites weren't very white and didn't stay white very long. They got dirty fast, as you can imagine, and as they were washed and worn they turned grayish, complementing the green well in the shadows of the forest.

"Major Simcoe exerted himself to preserve the Rangers in green, and to procure for them green waistcoats: his purpose was to wear the waistcoats with their sleeves during the campaign, and to add sleeves to the shell, or outer coat, to be worn over the waistcoats in winter: green is without comparison the best color for light troops with dark accoutrements; and if put on in the spring, by autumn it nearly fades with the leaves, preserving its characteristic of being scarcely discernible at a distance." [1]

Their green uniforms were deceptive in another way to unwary Colonials. In one episode, patrolling Ranger cavalryman Lt. Wickham was approached by two men from the woods who mistook him for a member of Continental Col. "Lighthorse" Harry Lee's cavalry, who wore green uniforms as well. Wickham cheerfully accepted the role bestowed him by the New Jersey committeeman and his friend.

Lt. Col. Simcoe had ridden well out in front with the Hussars to observe the ground ahead of his infantry and others who remained behind. Bringing along the two Americans, Wickham introduced Simcoe as Lee. Simcoe quickly accepted his role and played the part well. The two gave him, "the best account of the movements of the rebel army." The conversation ended when the committeeman asked, "I wonder what Clinton is about?" To which Simcoe replied, "You shall ask him yourself, for we are British." [1]

It wouldn't be the only time Simcoe passed the Queen's Rangers off as belonging to Lee's horse, and Lee himself admired Simcoe's pluck. At Richmond under Gen. Benedict Arnold, the Rangers approached a bridge destroyed by the militia who still occupied the territory. Some men of the militia approached Simcoe thinking he was Lee because of the green dress. Simcoe reprimanded them for not coming sooner and after his conversation with them, sent them back to Arnold as prisoners.

In this original drawing by Ranger Capt. Murray (subsequently colored in the early 1900s) the infantryman is shown with a short jacket and black accoutrements very similar to the rifleman's uniform (page 36) rather than the tailed coat many of today's paintings show. The Huzzar has a tall stovepipe shako and is armed with the Potter sword and pistols. Capt. Murray's drawings have been used to suggest the gear for the photos. Print courtesy the Toronto Public Library.

Rifles, Rangers & Revolution

Part II
Small Arms of the Rangers
Chapter 6
The Platypus Rifle

The unique muzzleloading P1776 rifle shared features with a musket.

THE MAJORITY of arms the Rangers bore were standard throughout the army, but the rifle—the first one made in England issued in quantity—had unique features not normally found in other rifles. Conceptually, the P1776 was designed from the beginning for use by infantry and cavalry. The only other British rifle sharing that claim is one of its most famous—the .303 Enfield No. 1 Mk III. After the P1776, cavalry would always be issued a carbine version of the infantry rifle.

British commanders, especially the Highlanders, had requested rifles before the war; an imperative when most American riflemen joined the revolt (the Continental army almost instantly raised 10 regiments of riflemen, and could've raised more). Rather than just buying rifles off shore as they had in the past, a trial led to the adoption of the rifle by gunsmith August Huhnstock of Hanover, Germany. Called the Pattern 1776, 200 were built in Hanover, and 800 of a slightly different version built by Birmingham gunsmiths (the one reviewed here). Both were rifled for the standard British .62 caliber carbine ball. The rifles arrived in America at the end of 1776 and one of the regiments issued them was the Queen's Rangers.

The P1776 was a well thought-out rifle, although the British version is more of a hodgepodge than the German version, since it appears to have a Brown Bess musket stock grafted onto a rifle's barrel. Shared features with the musket include a buttstock with the "handrail" style of comb, an apron behind the tang, and a forestock with the Bess' signature palm swell. Perhaps using a Bess pattern stock was the fastest way forward under the pressure of war.

The designers tried to include all the features a soldier might need for success either mounted or afoot on strange battlefields far away. Unfortunately, the 800 Birmingham rifles lacked the essential patchbox, although the 200 German rifles had one. The patchbox was considered important enough on a rifle that they aren't often left off even the meanest sporting rifles, but the Bess'

stock design isn't conducive to its inclusion.

The rifle is a handy 44¾ inches overall with a swamped, 28-inch barrel of .65 caliber. ("Swamping" means the barrel reaches its thinnest diameter about ⅔ the way up then enlarges toward the muzzle.) The listing of barrel calibers is a little sketchy. Today, we nominally call such a gun a ".62," since that is the minor size of the barrel's interior. (The military today uses the minor caliber of the bore when naming the cartridge rather than the groove size.) The bore of the original rifle measured for DeWitt Bailey's book measured .630 inch, with 8 grooves of .650 inch.[2] The nominal caliber of the issue carbine ball was 0.615 inch. I say nominal, because the caliber was determined by how many balls weighed a pound, and there were always minor variations.

The patch material couldn't be measured precisely either, and was calculated by the weight of a bolt of cloth, so the 0.015 between the 0.630-inch bore and 0.615-inch ball gave the soldier some leeway. Along with special powder, Hessians demanded linen patches, so it is likely British riflemen got the same. The P1776 rifle could also use the carbine ball wrapped in paper cartridges or even pistol cartridges in a pinch.

Sighting was accomplished with a 3-leaf backsight dovetailed into the barrel, and a brass blade foresight. Underneath the barrel is a complex, fragile system to contain the steel rammer used to seat the ball and clean the rifle.

The rammer, captured on the rifle by a swivel mechanism, is held in the stock by an external spring between the entry and middle pipes, and the spring is riveted to the entry pipe. Upon withdrawal, the swivels control the rammer as it rotates up and a pair of stop pins on either side of the muzzle arrest the movement, centering the rammer over the bore. The rod itself was held in the

The P1776 had a 3-leaf backsight drift adjustable for windage. Such a sophisticated aiming provision is a far cry from the simple bayonet stud used to point the Brown Bess! The brass-blade front sight is in a dovetail.

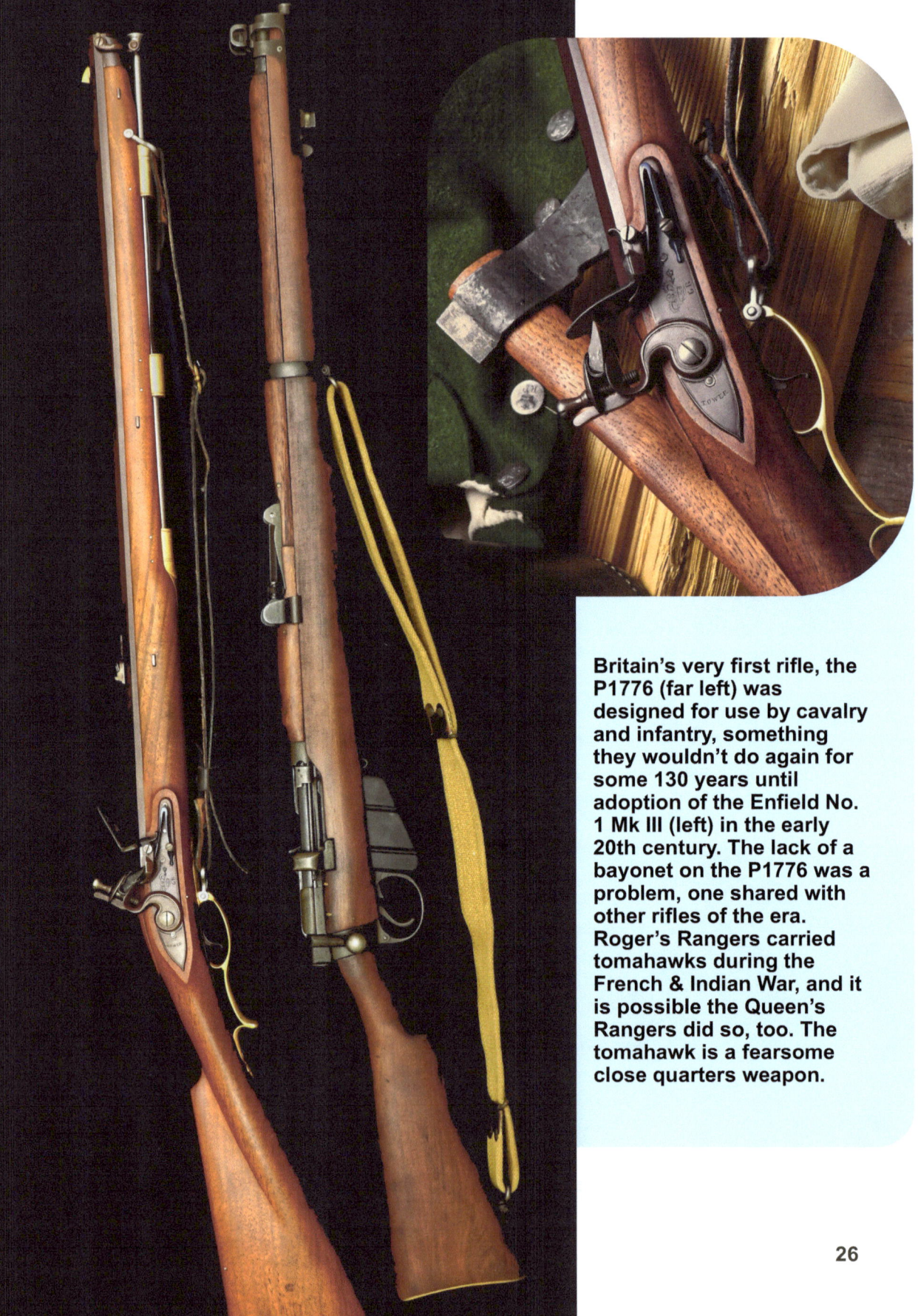

Britain's very first rifle, the P1776 (far left) was designed for use by cavalry and infantry, something they wouldn't do again for some 130 years until adoption of the Enfield No. 1 Mk III (left) in the early 20th century. The lack of a bayonet on the P1776 was a problem, one shared with other rifles of the era. Roger's Rangers carried tomahawks during the French & Indian War, and it is possible the Queen's Rangers did so, too. The tomahawk is a fearsome close quarters weapon.

swivels by a threaded brass nut. Removing the nut allows the rammer to be freed and then double as a cleaning rod with the appropriate tools threaded on. No tools survive that I can find, but these would likely be a ball puller and a worm for cleaning. A large, flat trumpet flare on the front of the rod assists driving the ball home, and would prove an asset in trying to draw a ball.

The chief benefit of this spring-captured rammer is it won't rocket out and get lost when used on horseback or carried upside down (the only comfortable way to sling the arm, by the way). The downsides are legion. The rod retaining spring is external, and could be damaged from a hard knock. The pins in the muzzle are small, and could be damaged during loading. If one of the nuts holding the swivel mechanism gets lost, the system fails. A plus, if the swivel system fails, the spring should still keep the rod in place.

The captured rammer on swivels gave the P1776 the versatility to be used on horseback and foot. To ease loading, the muzzle was swaged to admit a patched ball by finger pressure alone eliminating the short starter. Stop pins arrest the swivel arms and center the rammer over the bore. Little touches boosting the rifleman's speed in action.

Modern critics maintain these features were too complicated and delicate. This is true with the only caveat being that the rifle was not issued to recruits, but to veterans. The P1776's rammer system would be difficult to repair since there were so many small parts. Spare parts were likely scarce, since so few rifles were made in the first place, and the men issued them in small units. Still, the captured rammer gave the rifle the ability to be effective mounted or afoot. Whether the Mounted Rifles fired their rifles from atop a horse or fought like Dragoons by riding to the fight, dismounting and fighting on foot isn't mentioned in Simcoe's *Journal*, but they had a rifle giving them the option.

In writing about rifle-armed cavalry in his treatise, Ewald noted, "They have to be mounted and armed as light as hussars, only that each squadron has to have twenty-five good shots, armed with rifles, since those people are very useful on rearguards and in skirmishes. They can also be used in case a pass needs to be occupied and defended quickly, and the like." Ewald also notes that mounted rifles should be given the calmest horses available, and that they should practice firing from horseback. It is possible the Mounted Rifles trained to do both. It would be a useful skill.[14]

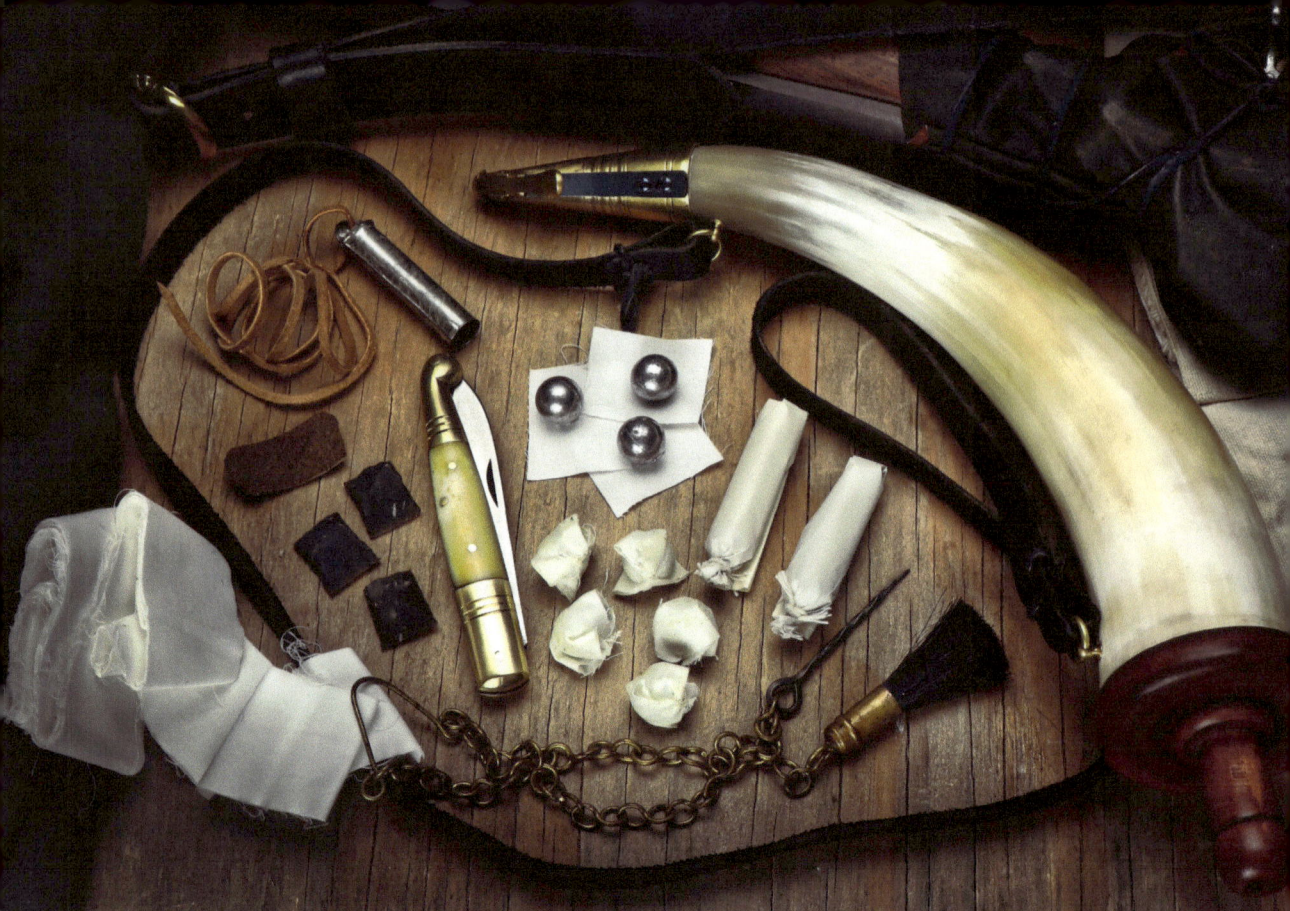

AMMUNITION FOR THE rifle took many guises, and was far more versatile than usually believed. Most varieties of ammo are shown corralled by the powder horn strap. The powder horn had no measure, so one of tin (above the knife) or a horn tip were common. Loose powder, patch and ball is slow to load, but time tested. Some methods sped things up.

Stitching the patch to the ball (just below the three roundballs) would make for a fast reload, and they could be greased ahead of time with tallow or sperm whale oil (plentiful and also used in lamps), or a dry one popped in the mouth and lubed with spit. Since the rifle used the same ball as the carbine, paper cartridges could be used in a pinch, even with coarse musket powder. The cartridge could be loaded like the musket cartridge—paper and all.

Cartridges were often made up on the battalion level, and these could be rolled around a ball with the patch stitched to it already, and filled with rifle powder. Either way kept all the components at hand in one piece, albeit a fragile one. Hessian riflemen insisted on linen patches, and a roll of linen (lower left) could be cut with a handy pocket knife. Some spare flints a spare bit of leather would keep the rifle sparking. The handy pick and brush on a chain is to keep the touch hole clear and debris swept from the flash pan.

Rifles, Rangers & Revolution

Chapter 7
Rifle Ammunition
An improved spin on versatility.

ON THE PRACTICAL side, the rifle designers also considered ease of loading. The muzzle of the P1776's iron barrel was swaged slightly larger so a patched ball could be seated flush in the barrel by finger pressure without using a mallet or short starter (one less gadget to carry and inventory). Today this method is called "coning the muzzle" and is done with a reamer or a hone, while back in the day when barrels were made of malleable iron, a mandrel could be pressed into barrel to gently swage it larger. Thus reloading was faster than usual with a conventional rifle, easing the task for the cavalryman. It was another premium step up in construction.

The P1776 was not equipped for a bayonet, although riflemen could have been issued short swords as a secondary weapon (that's what the Germans did). In lieu of a short sword, a tomahawk or hatchet may have been issued. The original Rogers' Rangers carried tomahawks, so it would be no surprise if riflemen of the Queen's Rangers carried them, since the unit was originally formed of Americans—some of them former Rogers' Rangers—who would have been quite aware of its value in close-quarters fighting. Generally, riflemen needed to be backed up by muskets, something Simcoe kept in mind as well.

DeWitt Bailey notes, "…what is not stated in the records is that much latitude was left to the individual riflemen and their officers as to how and with what their rifles were loaded." [3] Ammunition could be prepared in a variety of ways. First was loose patch and ball (the long-standing way to load a rifle). Among the known methods of preparing ammunition were stitching patches around balls, balls rolled into paper cartridges, and even the stitched-patch balls rolled into cartridges. This could be performed on an individual or company level, since they were secondary ways to load the arm and wouldn't be needed in volume.

Rolling the ball with a patch stitched to it into a paper cartridge gives the best of both worlds. That would be the best way to overcome a shortage of powder horns, too. It also is likely the carbine paper cartridges were used for emergency, and they would've been easy to get, even if the powder was coarser. Paper cartridges—where the ball uses the paper as a patch—shoot quite well from rifles for a short time. Even as accuracy falls off, your enemy is closing with you, so the higher volume of fire paper cartridges allow is a worthwhile trade, and easy to transition to.

Cloth patches need lubrication. Animal fat was easy to come by and tallow usually best, but goose or duck fat works well, as does sperm whale oil, widely used in lamps. Most common was spit, and if the ball was stitched to the patch, one could be popped in the mouth for a fast reload if it hadn't been pre-lubed with animal fat of some kind.

The riflemen were issued the same special "super fine, double strength" powder as the Jägers rather than coarse musket powder. The issue powder horn, which was likely the same as the one already issued to artillery, did not have a measure. Since German riflemen were expected to work up an accurate load for their individual pieces, British riflemen likely did the same. A simple measure could be made from a horn tip or by a tinsmith.

"Working up a load" would be different than the methods of modern handloaders, since scales to weigh charges were few and far between, and load workup with black powder has generous increments. The amount of powder needed to drive a ball was calculated by a fraction of the ball weight, and three were commonly used. Unlike smokeless powder, where fractions of a grain can make a big difference in performance, a black powder load (especially in these larger calibers) can be worked up in large increments as small as 5 grains or as large as 15. It just needs to be measured with consistency to shoot well.

A good comparison of the charges possibly used can be made using the Baker rifle (adopted in 1800) as a guide for which some documentation exists. We may find similarities, since it is the same caliber and the principles hadn't changed (haven't yet today, come to think of it). The service charge for the Baker rifle is listed by DeWitt Bailey as 110 grains, or just a little less than ⅓

The steel rammer was captured in the stock by a long spring running between the the entry pipe (held there by a rivet) and the middle pipe. The rammer was also kept to the gun by swivels and a feature giving it versatility for use mounted as well as afoot, since steel rammers can easily rocket out and be lost from horseback. Held by a brass nut, the rammer is removed for use as a cleaning rod, as shown here.

the weight of the ball, which was considered a maximum charge. A .62 roundball weighs 340 to 350 grains. The next two increments would be ¼ charge, or about 85 grains, and a ⅕ or 70 grains. I think it's safe to assume British riflemen used similar charges for their P1776 rifles, and I've had good luck with the ¼ charge. The 110-grain charge kicks pretty hard.

The Ferguson rifle gives us another example going in the opposite direction. It is charged with a little less than ⅕ charge, yet gives good accuracy using the same ball. I wouldn't be surprised to learn the expense of the "super fine, double strength powder" was such that lighter loads were encouraged in the muzzleloader.

Priming the pan presents some interesting options. When loading muskets, the pan was primed first with the paper cartridge, then the remainder poured into the barrel. Another option is explained by Hans Busk in *Hand-Book For Hythe* written in 1860, when he says, "…it was the custom to prime the musket from a flask containing powder of a still finer quality called 'serpentine powder,' but in the early flint lock musket, this proceeding was unnecessary, as in the act of loading, part of the charge passed through the touch-hole into the pan, when it was prevented from escaping by the hammer [frizzen]." (15)

The standard touchhole in military rifles of this era is 3/32 inch or so, which is rather large by modern standards. Today, they are smaller so even fine powder stays put when poured in, and you don't ignite your neighbor's whiskers or put his eye out with the jet of flame and debris blown out of the touchhole, since most folks shoot on ranges. (Putting a brass fence around the frizzen as reenactors do, or a shield on the shooting bench to prevent the side blast scorching your fellow shooter is the neighborly thing to do.) Large touch holes require use of a touchhole plug commonly done with the quill of a feather or a brass pin. Otherwise, powder as large as 1½ Fg may run out of the touchhole onto the ground when poured into the barrel.

As for the main charge pouring out the touchhole, the underside of the frizzen has a scallop where it faces the barrel to encourage the escape of powder, so it is a self-priming feature. Closing the frizzen and pouring a charge into the barrel primes the pan. When learning muzzleloading, old timers told me to slap the sideplate three times to "settle the powder, and the scallop encouraged faster ignition." This doesn't make sense to me now, since dropping the powder 30 inches or more easily settles it properly, and the pan flies open on firing. "Slapping" makes sense if you're ensuring the pan is primed. As an experiment, I loaded the rifle nine times in a row—three times each with FFFg, FFg and 1½ Fg with the frizzen closed, and the pan automatically primed each time.

Doing this creates a dangerous safety hazard, and I conducted my tests with the flint removed. But in a fight this certainly shortens the interval needed to fire the rifle, and would be even faster than loading a caplock. Paper cartridges load even faster. The other benefit is the pan is primed with the same amount of powder each time, and the main charge—important for consistent accuracy—would remain equally consistent. A criticism in the day of priming from the cartridge first was that the main charge was weakened too much and the balls fell short if the pan was accidentally overfilled when loading in haste. Of course, if the touchhole clogs, no priming reaches the pan, so the "belt and suspenders" approach would be to prime separately.

That the men of the Rangers trained with their rifles is evident, but sadly, the drill for rifles and how it differed from muskets, is lost. Simcoe offers the barest of clues, "The officers, commanding grand divisions, were ordered to make their men perfect in the whole of manual exercise. Sergeant M'Pherson, a corporal, and twelve men, were selected, and placed under the command of Lieutenant Shaw: they were armed with swords and rifles; and, being daily exercised in firing at objects, soon became most admirable and useful marksman." [1] The rifle is most likely the P1776, but whether the swords were the short infantry "hanger" type or Potter cavalry swords is not recorded. Since M'Pherson fought both as part of the Mounted Rifles and on foot, perhaps he and his men carried the cavalry saber issued to Loyalist units. They are longer than infantry hangers, but short enough not to drag on the ground when dismounted. One thing is for sure, small arms were in short supply for both sides, so they may have gotten a mix of everything.

The Rangers' Mounted Rifles were possibly equipped as Dragoons with Tarleton leather helmet, P1776 rifle, Potter saber and a belly box.

Chapter 8
Handling & Tactics
Employment of the P1776.

THE P1776 RIFLE weighs just 8½ pounds, having nearly neutral balance with just a hint of muzzle heaviness due to its swamped barrel. A common technique in muzzleloading days, the barrel reaches its narrowest at roughly ⅔ of its length, then flares back out larger at the muzzle, thus reducing weight and improving balance. The P1776 aims quite well, is compact, handy, easy to carry and fast into action. The 3-leaf backsight and brass blade front speak to its long-range ability. While "long-range" sights may sound optimistic, any hit from a lead sphere weighing some 340 grains would take an opponent off the field. Riflemen in those days routinely practiced at 200 yards and more.

While the sling swivels are in the normal position of a musket's—and the rifle is just as terribly uncomfortable slung muzzle up as is a musket—the rifle is very comfortable slung muzzle down, and the short barrel keeps the muzzle reasonably high off the ground. Another upscale touch, the P1776's forward swivel attaches to a plate affixed to the stock, and the sling does not have to be removed when dismounting the barrel. In all, the Pattern 1776 proved a very capable rifle, delivering accuracy, versatility and ease of care.

Thus armed and skilled, the Rangers were a capable corps, able to apply violence with precision. During the withdrawal from Elizabethtown Simcoe notes, "The riflemen of the Queen's Rangers, now commanded by Sergeant M'Pherson, were eminently distinguished on this retreat. The enemy's militia, who followed the army, were kept by them at such a distance, that very few shot reached the battalion; and they concealed themselves so admirably that none of them were wounded, whilst they scarcely returned a shot in vain." [1] The job of Light Infantry, and one where Riflemen excelled, was to move in the van, on the flanks, in the rear or all four during an army's marches.

Since they were slow to load and lacked bayonets, the rifles were normally backed up by men armed with smoothbores and fixed bayonets. Simcoe noted during one encounter, "There was some skirmishing between the Yagers [as his *Journal* calls them] and the enemy; and one time, it having the appearance of being serious, the Rangers were divided into two divisions, to march on each flank of the Yagers, who, having no bayonets, might have suffered from an intrepid enemy; but the contrary was the case, as the alarm originated from a shout that Captain Ewald, who commanded the rear guard, set up on the enemy's approach, which with other preparations, sent them away upon a full run.[1]

Ewald, had planned for such an event. In his treatise, he notes, "Since the loading of the rifles goes very slowly, the jäger in particular must be well taught that always one of two, or two of four, have loaded guns, so that they can support those who have fired already…

"If this maneuvre has to be performed during a retreat, one of the two, two of the four, or three of the six, retreat 50 to 100 paces after they have given fire, while the others save their fire until the retreated party has reloaded. This is the way how to retreat alternately. During all of this the officers and non-commissioned officers of the platoons have to constantly call to their men and give the necessary support so that the platoons do not get mixed up, causing disarray." [14]

As an aside, the Ferguson rifle eliminated these concerns, since it could be loaded and fired rapidly and mounted a bayonet. The tactics developed by Ewald were taken to heart by the Duke of York, head of the British army, and during the Napoleonic war, British riflemen, now armed with the new .62-caliber Baker rifle, learned to work in pairs and fire alternately for mutual defense. The Baker rifle also mounted a sword bayonet. Another lesson from the American Revolution taken to heart.

The P1776 had the features of a rifle from lock forward and of a musket back creating an odd (but effective!) platypus of a rifle. The flat sideplate is another sign of wartime economy. Earlier, it would likely have been much fancier.

Chapter 9
Traveling Light
Always prepared for action.

IN THE ONLY known period illustration of a Queen's Ranger rifleman by Ranger Capt. James Murray, the man is shown with rifle slung upside down, powder horn and possibly his haversack or pouch behind his back to carry ammunition, spare flints and other things necessary to run the rifle. He shows how lightly riflemen traveled, but sadly, the painting has little detail of the rifle or the accoutrements other than the horn, and we have to guess what's behind his back.

A belly box and belt might also have been worn, and would have been a natural accoutrement for the Mounted Rifles. One with a tin container rather than a cartridge block would be perfect for the various types of ammunition, spare flints, tools and a biscuit or two. Jackets in this era often had no pockets, not that pockets would last long stuffed with flints, balls, and other gadgetry necessary to keep a rifle running.

The belly box belt would be a good place for a rifleman afoot to hang a tomahawk, too. Simcoe's *Journal* makes little mention of hand-to-hand combat unless a bayonet is involved, so riflemen may have habitually run as light as Capt. Murray's painting shows. If not ranging far from the main body, and out for intelligence rather than mischief, the rifle and a few rounds may have been considered enough. Whether holding front or rear, shoot and scoot would have been the order of the day. Working as a sniper, the rifleman created a big cloud of smoke and it would behoove him to move.

Riflemen often acted as scouts ahead of the main party, or defended the rear on retreat. Their goal would be intelligence or a delaying action, not pitched battle. I can believe the rifleman pictured by Murray would have a half-dozen rounds or so stitched into patches for a fast reload. The riflemen would have been moving after shooting, and always moving toward the safety of the main body of the army if they encountered trouble. A fast reload would help keep things hot for the pursuit!

Another plus, the P1776 was easy to care for (or intended to be, that is). Instead of the barrel being pinned in place like the Brown Bess, it is fitted with a break-off breech and the barrel secured to the stock by three captured "slides" or "keys." (These were a feature usually found only on fine sporting rifles, but one the British military seemed to favor for rifles long after everyone else

Captain James Murray of the Queen's Rangers drew this picture of a Rifleman in the 1780s (subsequently colored around 1900) showing how lightly the men traveled. Note the rifle is slung upside down, and it is very comfortable to carry that way. Behind his back is perhaps a pouch for patches and balls. The original is in the Toronto Public Library.

switched to barrel bands.) After pulling these three keys, the barrel could be easily stripped out of the wood for cleaning while the keys stayed in the stock without chance of loss. The British normally used boiling water to clean black powder fouling (still a good way today) and being able to remove the barrel meant the wood wouldn't get soaked.

Rifles, Rangers & Revolution

Plug the touchhole, pour boiling water halfway up the barrel, put in the tompion and shake. Do that a few times and the barrel is clean. It takes longer if the water isn't hot. Dry out with tow waste and oil. It really isn't that simple, since fouling tends to get everywhere as anyone who shoots these arms knows. Black powder fouling is hygroscopic, and will absorb moisture from the air causing rust to form anywhere it is left unattended.

Tools like screwdrivers were only issued to sergeants as a rule and soldiers were rarely ever allowed to disassemble their arms. Rifles were so new it is likely the same orders about care as those for the Bess were used. These riflemen probably just cleaned their arms as best as they could without disassembly. It's not impossible, just messier and inconvenient. Standing orders for the Napoleonic War's Baker rifle expressly forbid removal of the lock except by "permitted men" in the presence of an officer or sergeant. It's likely riflemen were expected to clean their guns intact.

The Rifle Shoppe kits, like the one pictured here, are for advanced builders, and the only way to acquire one of these rifles, since only a couple have survived. Jess Melot, who made the molds for this kit noted the barrel was browned underneath the stock, but no finish remained on the external parts. While most British military arms of the era were issued "in the white" (meaning the metal left bare), this rifle was German designed, most of which were finished brown, and a brown finish would suit its mission far better than white. It is nearly impossible to shoot a rifle well if it's "in the white" since sunlight causes glare off the barrel. No record exists of how they were finished, but the fact brown finish survived under the barrel of the one the kit was made from convinces me they were browned.

The Pattern 1776 rifle set the bar high for British arms and exhibited a level of craftsmanship and engineering that carried on for another century in small arms design. The same level of craftsmanship was bestowed on the very next rifle—also called the Pattern 1776—designed by Major Patrick Ferguson. Its innovative engineering plus a new tactical doctrine should have led to success, but didn't.

Cleaning
Oh! What an odious chore!
However necessary, it wasn't easy or fun.

Care of the rifle (smoothbore, too, for that matter) was still in its infancy, but they didn't know that. Boiling water poured into the barrel and sloshed around worked surprisingly well, and still does. Block the touchhole, pour in water to fill ½ or ¾ of the barrel, cork the muzzle with the tompion (shown lower right) and shake. It can make a mess if you don't plug the touchhole well, but could be done without fieldstripping.

The P1776's rammer was withdrawn, and its brass stop nut unscrewed. The rod could be removed from its swivel, and a "patch worm" (under the muzzle) made of twisted iron ending in two sharp points threaded on. The tow, which came in a little bundle, was twisted around the worm and run into the bore to

scour out what was left of the detritus, dry, and then oil with sperm whale oil. Sperm whale oil is a long-proven, highly effective lubricant/preservative and a little tin oil bottle (next to the muzzle) was made to fit into a cartridge block hole of the cartridge box. (Only in the last couple of decades have other types of oils come close to the properties whale oil has naturally.) Any oil was used in a pinch but whale oil worked best.

Behind the oil bottle is the common musket tool issued to sergeants. Sergeants of the regular infantry were responsible for ensuring every man had a fresh flint in his arm before battle, but riflemen were different. The nature of those entrusted with rifles meant they were a cut above the rest, since they often worked independently, so it wouldn't be surprising to find riflemen in charge of their pieces and keeping a simple turnscrew handy, if not the big sergeant's tool.

Tow waste (middle), the byproduct of making linen cloth from the flax plant, was the 18th century's idea of today's cleaning patch. Living up to its name "waste," tow leaves behind little pieces of itself down in the chamber area (and all over the gear and gun during photography). Very flammable, tow was also used to start fires with flint and steel. Firing the first round could leave smoldering embers of tow down near the touchhole, which could ignite the next charge poured down. Blowing down the muzzle between shots extinguished these embers in addition to keeping the fouling soft (putting your mouth over a gun muzzle is something giving rangemasters the vapors today, but was something I was taught to do when I started shooting in the 1970s). This is also why a powder charger was (and still is) used. An original rule of shooting muzzleloaders was to never load from the horn, an eternal lesson still true today. Practitioners of the rule usually have all their fingers.

In the foreground is the pick and brush meant to be worn in a button hole and used to keep the touchhole clear and the pan swept of debris. A plugged touchhole is an obvious cause of misfires, but fouling in the flash pan led to slower ignition as fouling built up, so brushing the pan was a necessary act to perform regularly even under combat conditions.

The tompion shown is a just a cork with a loop added. It is a simplified version of one seen in the frontispiece of *Scloppeteria*, a book written in 1808 by a former Captain of the 95th Rifles. Much of the loading information comes from his chapters on shooting. And the pipe? Not necessary for cleaning the rifle, but a pleasant distraction performing the drudgery of a soldier's endless chores.

Chapter 10
The Ferguson Rifle
A truly "revolutionary" concept!

WHILE THE P1776 muzzleloading rifles were being completed and shipped, British ordnance received another order for 100 very unusual rifles that probably couldn't have changed the course of the war, but would have revolutionized small arms in future wars had the innovative tactics and rifles been nurtured.

These were also called Pattern 1776 Rifles, normally with the name of the inventor Capt. Patrick Ferguson added. Their fame has driven the preceding P1776 rifle out of the limelight almost entirely. They are held up as ultimate secret weapons or derided as impossibly expensive vanity toys. The truth is stranger.

Patrick Ferguson is often denigrated today because he didn't really invent the rifle bearing his name (despite having patents) and its tactical superiority largely unproven. A turning-breech rifle had been available to discriminating sportsman for quite some time already. The Board of Ordnance even toyed with such a design as early 1762 for specialist troops, having gone to the trouble of ordering 25 built.[2] So this wasn't new, unproven technology, just never perfected. Ferguson's improvement gave the rifle the ability to better manage the fouling of the powder for sustained, rapid fire, something essential to a military rifle. He is also credited with the tapered chamber centering the ball into the rifling, and added the bayonet other rifles eschewed.

The construction has some unique points. The Ferguson shares a stock design very similar to the P1776 muzzleloader, and the Brown Bess parentage of both becomes patently obvious side-by-side. The grip rail buttstock is present, there is no patchbox (the Ferguson of all rifles doesn't really need one),

Left: The Ferguson rifle was fast and simple to load. Drop a greased ball into the chamber, push it forward, pour powder behind it and raise the breech. Excess powder can be swept into the pan for ignition, and the chamber depth controls the powder charge. Fewer gadgets are necessary to run these rifles. Unlike other rifles that become hard to load and less accurate the more they are fired, the Ferguson shoots accurately and is not sensitive to fouling. With the threads on the screw properly greased, the gun shoots far longer than conventional rifles. Left bare, seven to 12 accurate shots can be fired before the screw becomes too difficult to turn and its fouling must be addressed.

THE FERGUSON RIFLE added the much needed bayonet military theorists had long criticized other rifles for lacking. The overall length of the rifle and bayonet was similar to contemporary muskets like the Brown Bess or French Charleville (its chief opponent). Whereas musket bayonets were mostly useless off the firearm, and only good as thrusting weapons when affixed, the 24-inch-long Ferguson bayonet had a long enough handle it could be used as short sword in a pinch. The Ferguson blade had a long fuller running down the center, and was sharpened on both sides. Ferguson taught his men to slash at their opponent's hands with the blade while bayonet fighting. Note the front sight of the Ferguson is not the bayonet lug, which on the Bess also served as an aiming reference. The Ferguson bayonet lug is on the bottom of the barrel. Neither the Bess or Ferguson had bayonet locks, and the bayonets could be accidentally detached when least desired during the rather gruesome twisting and tugging of a bayonet action.

The common 29-shot cartridge box worn slung over the shoulder on a crossbelt had a tin tray under the wooden block. It wouldn't surprise me to find Ferguson simply plucked out the wooden block and used the tin tray for the rifle's ammo. The Ferguson only required greased balls, powder horn and flints to work. The third compartment of the tray could house tow waste and its worm. The Ferguson rifle is far simpler to operate than a musket. These .615-inch roundballs are greased with a 2:1 mixture of beeswax/mutton tallow.

and the forearm has the nifty bulge for the left hand. The barrel is held with three keys or "slides" and the rammer pipes are very similar to the P1776 muzzleloader (both quite different from the Brown Bess).

A wooden rod is present rather the steel rod usually found at this time on British military arms. Jess Melot mentioned the rod on the original gun was an old replacement and no original survives. The Rifle Shoppe rods are copied from the one aboard the original with the exception of a brass rather than horn rod head. Jess felt no military rifle would use horn, and this rod also has a plain tail. Likely the tail had a fixture to hold a worm or other cleaning tool. Steel rammers were specified for their durability in service, but the Ferguson didn't need one to load for combat, just for cleaning and unloading, so wood would work fine and keep the cost down. Jess also found the original barrel had been browned and varnished upon removing it from the wood.

The lock is substantially smaller than the musket lock and similar in size and operation to the P1776 muzzleloader, but they are not interchangeable in size or parts. The trigger is pinned to the wood and the pull crisp but heavy at 7 pounds. The rifle itself weighs 9 pounds, 9 ounces. The balance point is right

"PF" over a crown was Patrick Ferguson's mark stamped at the back of the screw. Just below on the flat is the "Crown/Crossed Scepter" proof, and forward of that MB & IW" for makers Matthias Barker and James Whately.

under the rear sight, and the rifle holds and aims very nicely offhand. The rear sight has one fixed leaf, and one very tall folding leaf. The front sight is sweated onto the barrel far enough back to allow the bayonet to be affixed. The bayonet lug is sweated on underneath the barrel. The round, tapered 33-inch barrel isn't very thick or heavy and the balance closer to the action due to the heavy screw-breech, but the rifle holds very well for offhand shooting.

The sling swivels are sufficiently odd enough for comment. The rear swivel is affixed to the side of the stock where it is strongest, and keeps the sling out of the way for loading. The swivel is mounted to a square stud set into the wood at a slight downward angle, and a pin driven through it from the top. The swivel itself is free to move on one axis only, and does not rotate.

The front swivel is odd being a simple half-round loop rather than a flat loop that would conform to the shape of the sling as used on the other P1776 and Brown Bess. It is a style of sling swivel mostly found on rifles of Germanic origin. A screw passes through the wood securing it, and the sling may be left in place when dismounting the action from the stock.

Right: The 2-foot-long Ferguson socket bayonet (top) had a long enough socket to wield as a sword, and was sharpened full length on both sides. Round handles on swords and knives are difficult to control, however, and British designers took this to heart. The next rifle issued, the P1800 Baker (bottom) had a 23-inch-long sword bayonet with a brass handle and guard more sure in the hand. The Baker bayonet fitted to a sturdy bar brazed to the barrel and held by a spring lock (note the spring atop and button below the handle) to address the habit the socket style had of slipping off rifle if it is twisted during its withdrawal from the unfortunate on the other end. The Baker bayonet was only sharpened about five inches from the tip. This no doubt kept riflemen from razoring themselves open on loading—not a problem with the Ferguson—but likely the major reason few other rifles had bayonets.

Patrick Ferguson, his namesake rifle and 100 men were assigned to the Queen's Rangers upon their arrival in America. Unluckily for military science—but lucky for the fledgling country in rebellion—Ferguson was wounded before encountering Lt. Col. Simcoe and Capt. Ewald, since all three were serious students of tactics. Patrick Ferguson was an inventor in addition to being a tactician. Ewald and Simcoe made a dynamic contribution to Light Infantry tactics, and the inclusion of Ferguson's ideas and his new breechloading rifle may have inspired seminal change. His unit was too small to be of consequence to a grand army but perfect for the small unit tactics of the Rangers, where his concepts could be assessed and refined by like minded men. His rifle could have revolutionized warfare if employed on a grander scale, especially after being perfected by experience and with tactical theories honed with the input of men like Simcoe and Ewald.

His rifle was never improved beyond its early development, and his tactical theory never explored. It is often said the British despised riflemen, but they only despised riflemen shooting at them. They had no problem with their riflemen returning fire. Despite the noise about the British denigrating the rifle as impractical, commanders in America appreciated rifles and understood the special how and why of their use. After all, Britain brought over 4,000 Hessian riflemen—Jägers—and built 1,000 rifles for use by their own Light Infantry.

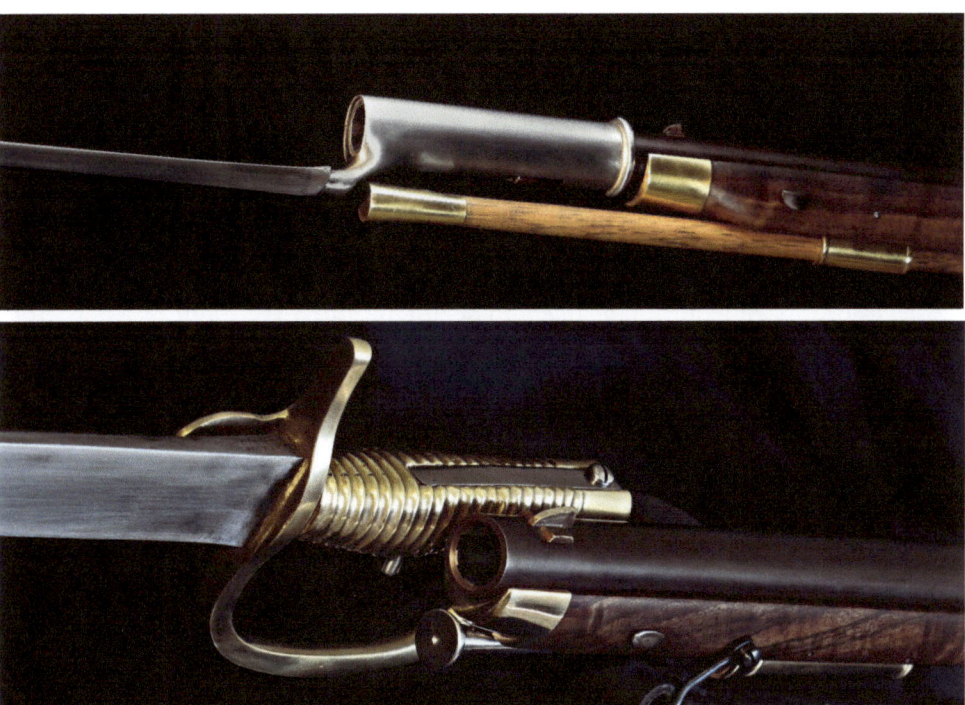

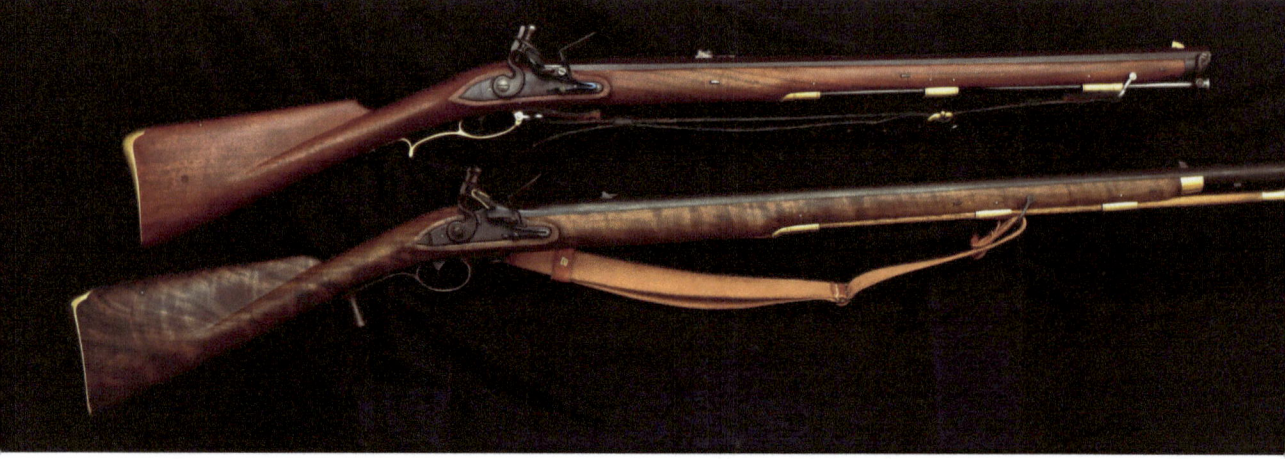

Not surprisingly, because they were made so close together in time, both P1776 rifles share some common design features. Both have Brown Bess style stocks, similar rod pipes and similar, if not interchangeable, locks. Both were built by the same contractors.

Rifles were not unwelcome or misunderstood. The concept of rifle use by Light Infantry went hand in hand, and had been well appreciated since before the French & Indian War in America when commercial rifles were issued.

Captain Ferguson's ideas centered on the rifle not only as a skirmish weapon, but one that could replace the musket as a line infantry weapon. His concept was for the line to open with accurate, aimed fire while beyond range of reply. His men could load and deliver this aimed, accurate fire from prone, too, where they were far less vulnerable to artillery. The Ferguson rifle could be loaded prone easily unlike conventional muskets and rifles. Trained riflemen could fire up to seven shots a minute. Although aim suffers with speed, speed counts more as the opposition closes in. Ferguson personally demonstrated his shooting in front of the King at ranges out to 300 yards. He put all his shots on the 100-yard target with five in the bull's-eye, according to eyewitnesses. All this in a rainstorm on a windy day as well!

From the rifle's maximum range, hits from the return musketry of the smoothbore would have been an accident, and a regiment of riflemen lethal to opposing infantry, and equally hazardous to cavalry. The rifle and its 2-leaf sight was capable of putting a ball on a man out to 300 yards in Ferguson's hands. That's a long way for an opponent to walk under fire.

Unlike conventional rifles, the Ferguson could maintain this accurate fire far longer, and as the opposition marched closer, the Ferguson's lethality remained constant where a conventional rifle's would decrease as it fouled, first robbing accuracy, then fouling beyond the ability of the man to load easily, and then fouling beyond the ability to load at all. Where the smoothbore could deliver 20 shots or more before fouling out, the muzzleloading rifle was lucky to reach five or seven. With properly greased balls and breech screw the

Ferguson continues firing. The downside would be grease melting off the balls during hot days, and clumping together over cool nights.

The addition of a 24-inch sword bayonet increased the Ferguson-armed riflemen's versatility. No other rifles were fitted with bayonets until the Napoleonic War when Britain added a bayonet to the P1800 Baker. It, too, mounted a sword bayonet, and it's hard to believe the lesson of the Ferguson wasn't used in the decision to choose that style.

Another forsaken aspect of the Ferguson's firepower was the ability of two or three ranks to maintain continuous rapid fire from prone, kneeling and standing. A smaller unit would have the ability to engage larger ones with rapid, lethal firepower, something not practical until the metallic cartridge arrived. As skirmishers, they could make things hot for artillery, too, and well beyond range of all but artillery.

The Ferguson is safer. Muzzleloaders often have embers burning in the breech area from the previous shot unless the shooter wipes or blows down the muzzle. A subsequent load can be ignited with dire consequences to the hand at the muzzle, or detonating the horn if the shooter is unwise enough to load from one. By opening the breech the embers are quickly extinguished, and there are no combustible materials like paper to smolder. Finally, the rifle is primed *after* it is loaded, unlike other British arms which were primed first.

The 2-leaf rear sight (left) has a fixed open notch and a very tall standing leaf for the considerable drop of the 344-grain roundball over the modest charge of powder. Ferguson found less powder gave better accuracy with the added benefit of spraying less hot gas into the shooter's face. The front sight (right) is a simple shark fin blade soldered to the barrel. The rear sight is drift adjustable for windage. (The "FR" button is just a guess, No originals are known.)

 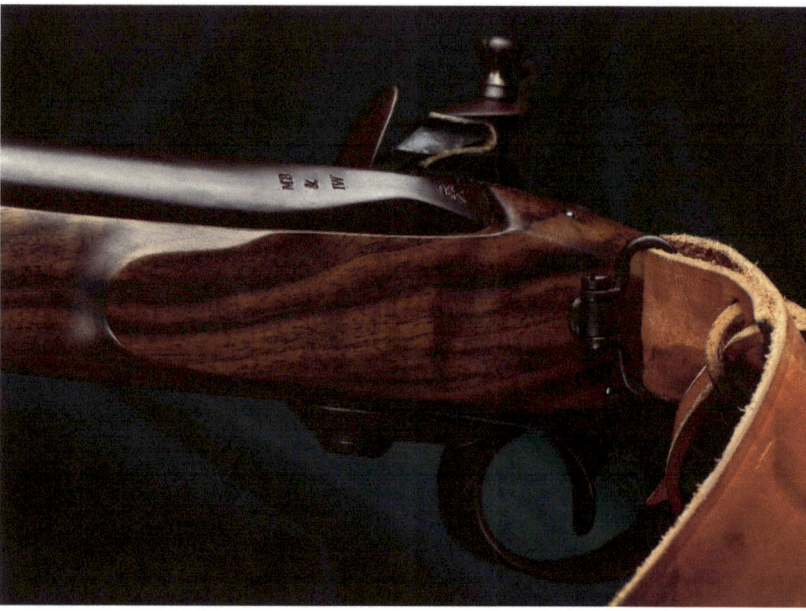

The front sling swivel follows the German Jäger rifle's "U"-shape (unlike the other P1776's Bess style swivels), and the rear swivel is an odd duck entirely. The rear swivel is on a square post carefully inlet into a square hole *on an angle*, then secured with a pin running top to bottom. The swivel only "swivels" left to right. The left stock panel is bare and undecorated, another unusual touch for an 18th century arm.

The Ferguson bayonet's socket was made longer than the standard bayonet so the men could wrap their hand around it for use as a sword if necessary. Another aspect of the Ferguson bayonet was it was sharpened on both edges. Ferguson taught his men to slash at an opponent's hands while fencing. Regular bayonets were thrusting weapons only. The Ferguson added slash to the thrust. The later Baker bayonet had a sword handle and guard.

What remains in the records of Ferguson's original orders aren't very clear on the aims and goals of the exercise he wanted to pursue. In his letter to General Howe, Secretary at War Lord William Barrington vaguely states, "[Ferguson] having by Directions from the Board of Ordnance superintended the making of some Riffle Barrel pieces of a new Construction, the King has thought it proper to order that experiment should be made in the most proper manner as to their Utility."

It's possible Ferguson was able to explain his vision to Howe upon his arrival in America. Gen. Howe was a proponent of the Light Infantry, and Ferguson attended Howe's school on Light Infantry in 1774, where he excelled and likely began forming many of his ideas. However, Ferguson's Corps of 100 was such a small contingent, they mattered little in the bigger schemes of battle. They could only prove themselves working in one of the smaller units.

Rifles, Rangers & Revolution

Howe picked the one unit where Ferguson could prove himself—under the command of Maj. Wemyss of the Queen's Rangers (along with Capt. Ewald's Hessian riflemen), and all engaged in the Battle of Brandywine on September 11, 1777. There, Ferguson and the Rangers acquitted themselves well and received commendation from Gen. Howe.

Brandywine is where Ferguson famously passed up a shot at Gen. George Washington accompanied by Brig. Gen. Casimir Pulaski. He eschewed shooting them in the back as they rode away or the history of this country might be very different today. Whether it is true is open to speculation, since the story was pieced together after the battle while Ferguson was being treated for his wounds. He put two and two together hearing a description of Washington and Pulaski.

Ferguson was severely wounded—shot through the right elbow—and there the promise of the Ferguson rifle ends, as Ferguson never really recovered from his wound. He learned to write and shoot left-handed, since his right arm healed crooked (and was almost amputated). Ferguson would be killed at King's Mountain October 7, 1780, and his rifle's potential buried with him.

No real clear explanation for the dissolution of his rifle company has ever arisen. Rifle use was on the rise in the British Army. Ferguson's men and non-commissioned officers were drawn from units posting to America along with Ferguson, and were sent back to their units upon dissolution of his company. There is evidence they took their rifles along.

Often, rifle companies were detached in squads to line infantry companies, since they could be used to cover movement with their unique ability to apply violence so much farther away. In boat landings, riflemen would be out of the boat first. (Ferguson's Corps were among the first off the boat leading up to the Battle of Brandywine.) Off first, they could secure the beachhead and begin scouting for the enemy, key roles for light infantry.

It is very possible Howe treated them as he might any other rifle company by breaking them up into smaller groups. Many Highlander rifle companies were used this way, too. The Hessians usually moved in companies, since they had an added language barrier. Had Howe understood the unique capabilities of the rifle, it is possible he would have reacted differently. Or maybe not. There were now less than 100 of them, by design they were on loan from their original units, their officer severely wounded, and certainly no way to test the more grandiose of Ferguson's ideas. But there was a real need for trained riflemen throughout the army, and here were 100 rifles that could do more good dispersed back to their former units than kept idle awaiting their officer's recovery—if he recovered at all.

Chapter 11
The Paoli Massacre

A squad of Ferguson's Rifles springs a bloody surprise.

FERGUSON WAS NOTIFIED soon after Brandywine that his company was being disbanded. There is one last recorded instant of their appearance, but the riflemen were unable to show off their value and never fired their rifles. On the evening of September 20, 1777 Major General Charles Grey led a surprise attack on Mad Anthony Wayne's encampment near the Paoli Tavern (Washington left Wayne behind to act as a buffer and to harass the British rear while he moved the main army). This was a bayonet action, and Grey ordered arms to be unloaded and flints removed in order to maintain surprise. Wayne's casualties amounted to more than 250 men killed, wounded and captured compared to Grey's casualties of 11. The lopsided nature of the action led to the American press calling it a "massacre." This was a victory in the British eyes, as Wayne was routed, but Washington got the main army away.

At the battle it is noted riflemen were in the van, and used their "Rifleman's Swords" to dispatch the sentries. A squad of what appear to be Ferguson's riflemen are depicted in the 1782 painting by Xavier della Gatta. The painting was commissioned by two British officers who participated in the attack, and they corrected the artist's work to accurately reflect who was there. The presumed squad of five Ferguson's riflemen are shown in green jackets with feathered hats pinned up on one side. They're holding guns with extremely long bayonets mounted underneath rather than on the side as with the Brown Bess muskets pictured nearby (which are shown with shorter bayonets).

While della Gatta's skill won't make us forget Da Vinci anytime soon, he is trying to accurately portray and define the participants. The poor draftsmanship doesn't mask the fact the artist is trying his best to get the

The Battle of Paoli is one of the more gruesome actions of the Revolutionary War. The British were successful in a surprise attack on Mad Anthony Wayne's men as they slept using bayonets only. Major General Grey had the flints removed from the arms (to ensure an accidental shot wouldn't raise an alarm) rendering the capabilities of the rifle moot. Riflemen were said to have dispatched Wayne's piquets, and here the long sword bayonet proved its worth.

picture correct in the details. He had the input of two officers who were present, and it was painted close to the actual time of the battle. It is no accident he adds a squad of British soldiers dressed in green who have arms with bayonets under the muzzles among the other squads wearing red and carrying arms with shorter, side-mounted bayonets of the Brown Bess. Also interesting is four of the five men have "white" crossbelts, while the 5th appears to have black crossbelts. This may indicate the men were equipped with gear assembled rather higgledy-piggledy!

Black accoutrements were commonly issued to Light Infantry, whether in red or green tunics. The "white" crossbelts (not really white, but more like an off white) would be more commonly available than black and, based on the painting, it's possible after Ferguson was wounded, any of his men may needing new accoutrements used what their new company gave them. It supports the notion Howe broke them up into small units rather than disbanding them.

Don Troiani paints his Ferguson Rifleman with natural leather belts. Ferguson put his plans together in England, where the infantry uniform color was universally red with white buff crossbelts. The Hesse-Kassel Jägers wore natural leather belts over their green jackets and Ferguson may have modeled his men's uniform color and accoutrements after these Hessian riflemen, since such colors were better suited to the scouting part of a rifleman's skills. Ferguson took along enough green cloth to uniform his men once in America. Since the front sling swivel of the rifle is of the Germanic style, it follows other influences of the Jäger may appear in the uniforms, too.

Chapter 12
What Became of the Fergusons?
The rifles and the men vanish from memory.

HOWE ORDERED FERGUSON'S men returned to their regiments. Since they were volunteers, they had been detached for service with Ferguson prior to their departure from England, and still carried on the rolls of their original regiments, all of whom also came over on the same ship. Perhaps we can offer a different ending for the rapid-firing Ferguson rifle than the commonly-held belief that British disdain for rifles sidelined them, or that a peevish Howe revenged himself for having these men shoved into his command by dismissing them out of hand.

Indian fighting and the French & Indian War showed the value of rifles and light troops. The army long used riflemen as scouts, but lost almost all of them to the rebel cause. Rifles purchased for that conflict had been used up and not replaced. Because of this real need for rifles, I believe the Ferguson riflemen were quickly dispersed with their rifles, since they were already trained. New riflemen take some time to become proficient. I suggest Ferguson's men were sent back to their Regiment's Light Companies in the manner the British planned for other riflemen. If this is true, then the rifles were either disabled by indifference or simply used up in service. Likely, the original allotment came with few—if any—spare parts, and repairs would have been problematic. As they broke down, they would've been replaced with the muzzleloading P1776, or even a musket.

The Ferguson rifle was stronger than it looked, yet will suffer greatly from indifferent care. The stock was particularly susceptible to damage during removal of the action, yet that is the best way to give it a thorough cleaning. In those days, however, men were discouraged from disassembling their arms, and I believe it likely Ferguson's men weren't excepted from this policy. The Ferguson isn't conducive to disassembly in the field. It requires removal of the tang screw, and all three slides, whereas the muzzleloading P1776 had a break-off breech to ease barrel removal.

The Ferguson would be a difficult rifle to clean in the stock with all the nooks and crannies where fouling accumulates. It's a difficult rifle to clean even with today's far better tools. The boiling water method would still work magic on the gun, but it's hard to see how the stock wouldn't get a good soaking. Poor cleaning would provide another avenue for failure down the line. During

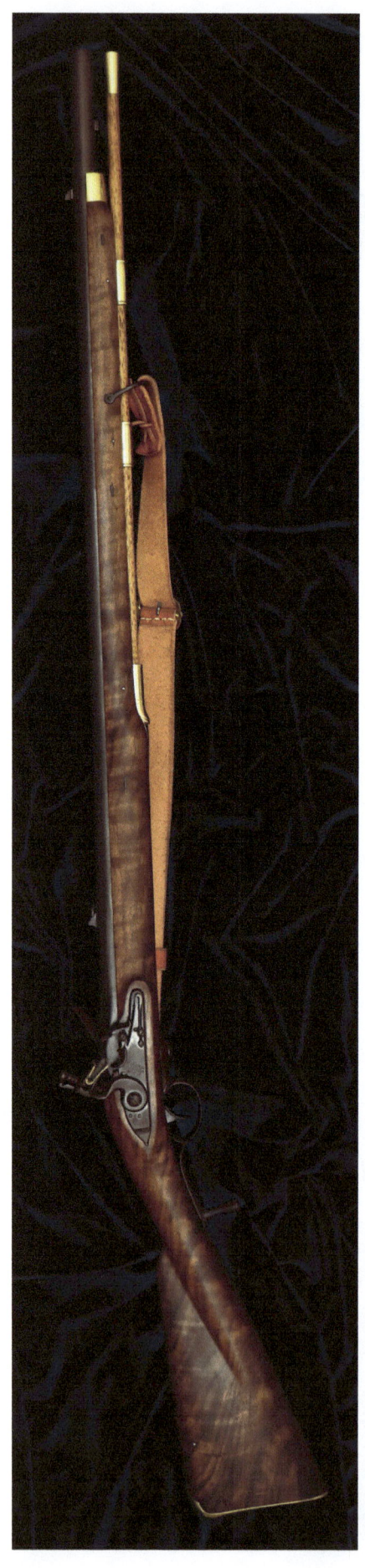

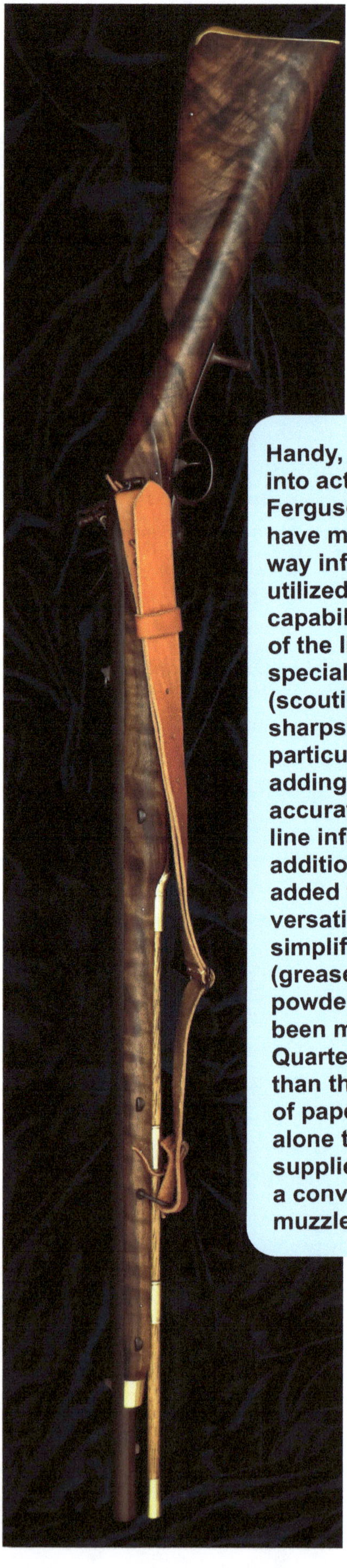

Handy, light and quick into action, the Ferguson rifle should have modernized the way infantry were utilized with its capability of handling all of the light infantry's specialty chores (scouting and sharpshooting in particular) in addition to adding devastatingly accurate firepower in the line infantry role. The addition of the bayonet added to the rifle's versatility, and the simplified ammunition (greased ball and powder) should have been much easier for the Quartermaster Corps than the tedious rolling of paper cartridges let alone the additional supplies required to run a conventional muzzleloading rifle.

disassembly, the natural impulse is to use the barrel for leverage, and that *will* result in the stock breaking.

Many say the stock is weak and prone to failure because it's bored through for the action, but any mishaps sidelining the Ferguson would equally sideline other arms. The Ferguson is just as strong or stronger than the other P1776 and Brown Bess, since there is metal all the way through the center of the gun. Left together and carefully cleaned, it should last as long as the others.

The big difference affecting maintenance is there were only 100 to begin with. Loss or combat damage to any of the main parts would sideline the rifle, especially the stock, which would require the efforts of a skilled gunmaker. The only (mostly) complete original Ferguson has iron straps reinforcing the stock broken through at the action.

If any of the parts peculiar to the rifle were damaged or lost, the rifle would be put out of action. One relic supporting this is a triggerguard dug up in New York. It fell off after the screw holding it to the breech-screw fell out.

The breech-screw itself could be lost in action. Mine fell out at the range under controlled circumstances while I was learning how to use the rifle. I tilted the rifle with the breech-screw turned out and it unscrewed the rest of the way and fell on the table. I could imagine that happening while cannon balls were whizzing by along with a volley of musket fire. Some may have been captured and survived the war only to be broken accidentally in untutored hands and scrapped.

The gun is susceptible to the breech screw fouling to the point it becomes impossible to work. Without Ferguson to maintain a cleaning regimen, some men may have gotten sloppy. Finally, the ammunition requires extra effort (see Chapter 30). The breech threads and balls need to be lubed with beeswax or beeswax/tallow to deliver the stellar performance Ferguson achieved with the rifle. Even had the squads under a corporal, sergeant or lieutenant been able to explain what they needed, it may have fallen on deaf ears or been beyond the belief of their new officers or a surly quartermaster. The technology was that new. The thought of providing just a squad with special ammunition could have irritated a higher up more concerned with the next action.

Ones not used up in service were probably traded in for the other P1776, since it was technology everyone understood, and the Fergusons scavenged for parts and scrapped. It is also likely if one or two guns became disabled, the men were ordered to turn in all their Fergusons for the muzzleloader so everyone had the same rifle and ammunition. No rifles went back to England, so it's possible they were all destroyed before the British left, rather than leaving them for the Americans.

Ferguson designed his uniform and gear in England. Only the painting of the Battle of Paoli shows the uniform to any degree, and the group of men are small. Ferguson mentions "tann'd leather" and it is possible he patterned his gear after the German Jägers who wore green jackets and natural leather belts. Such subdued colors match the mission of the Light Infantry well. The cartridge box is overly large, yet Ferguson only had 100 men and very probably chose from patterns for existing accoutrements. The bayonet scabbard follows existing doctrine with brass throat and chape over wood-lined black leather. Belts are by Jim Keller, scabbard by Tritonworks, hat and sling by C&D Jarnigan.

Chapter 13
Ferguson's Promise Lost
"What Might Have Been…"

WITHOUT FERGUSON, the wonderful tactical concepts he wove died, since he was never able to fully demonstrate his rifle's superiority in action after Brandywine. Sad fact is, nascent, unproven technology needs development to improve, and that requires a commitment. Jess Melot, who created the reproduction Ferguson kit, examined another, later version of the screw breech with the screw offset forward. This eliminated the blowback of gas into the shooter's face, one of the big detractions of the Ferguson.

Even before the end of the Revolution, creative minds were at work on the sundry problems. With Ferguson gone, there was no one to pick up the pieces. I liken it to sending John Northrop up in a P-51 Mustang to fight Messerschmitts then declaring the plane no good after he is shot down and killed. Without Ferguson to promote the tactical concepts, his rifle died. While some argue the Ferguson was too expensive, all rifles were expensive, far more costly than a musket. A better argument is the military establishment wouldn't think it possible the average soldier could be trained to use one. Attitudes towards the competence and value of the common soldier were low, since most were uneducated. This wouldn't improve until the Napoleonic Wars, when the observation of the 95th Rifles in action led to a better understanding of the value of a highly trained private.

Even with an appreciation of the value of Ferguson's invention, it wouldn't be in time to prove of more than marginal value in the Revolution. Besides, the American Revolution was decided more by movement than force of arms or technology. Cornering Cornwallis and forcing his surrender at Yorktown was pivotal.

As for highly trained troops, even in the Napoleonic Wars British high command seemed to wield such units as would a 6-year-old given a finely tuned target handgun—like a hammer. The 95th Rifles were often sent off on strange missions costing considerable men due to poor planning and an incomplete understanding of what missions best utilized their skills. Snipers in WWII were treated the same way until generals were convinced to attend briefings on how to use them. Then snipers began to excel in their craft (for gathering intelligence as well as delivering violence). Nothing like that happened in the Revolution (fortunately for America).

Ferguson and his rifle were truly revolutionary. Both Ferguson and Lt. Col. Simcoe were tactical theorists, but never met, since Simcoe didn't take over the Rangers until a month after Ferguson was wounded. Throw into the mix doctrine practiced by Hessian Capt. Johann von Ewald, whose post-war book helped modernize the British Army under the Duke of York's tutelage, and a revolution in military thinking may have arrived a lot sooner.

It would have been interesting to see how Simcoe played his "Ferguson card" in some Ranger battles. I believe Simcoe would have been open to the innovative use of the rifle as a line-infantry firearm hoodwinking his opponent into thinking things were going off normally until too late. No one was better at pulling off a joke on an opponent, and the Ferguson would have given him new possibilities for the "chicanery of war."

The world is probably lucky the three never connected. Had they perfected the way the breechloader could be used, and a perfected breechloader adopted by the world's militaries, carnage like that of U.S. Civil War and WWI would have occurred much earlier. Used by the likes of Napoleon Bonaparte, much more mischief would've engulfed the world were an accurate breech-loading rifle (not to mention a breech-loading cannon) the standard. Napoleon caused enough death, destruction and misery with smoothbore muzzleloaders.

However, the Ferguson was not forgotten. The U.S. M1819 Hall rifle was a breechloader, and it served all the way through the Civil War to good effect. The Hall also used a modest charge to drive its .52-caliber ball, and was known for good accuracy (as well as spraying hot gas in the shooter's face). It's not hard to believe Hall's inspiration was the Ferguson rifle.

Perhaps earlier widespread use of a breech-loading rifle is an example of Divine Mercy. Napoleon went adventuring in Russia as Pauly was inventing centerfire cartridge ammunition in Paris in 1812. The world was spared once again massive carnage if only for a time. God works in mysterious ways!

As it was, the stinging nettle of the American Revolution left the Crown scrambling for income, and there was nothing left to pursue dreamy technological advancements or even blasé ones like a new muzzleloading rifle to replace all the ones lost. That would change when the people of France revolted and that little Corsican artilleryman became Consul, declared himself Emperor, and launched another World War to begin the 19th century. Britain's third rifle—the Baker—proved to be the best rifle of the Napoleonic War—and as sharp a thorn in the side of the French as the American long rifle was to the British in 1776.

The breech screw only requires one revolution to open. Upon closing, the lever slides into a recess cut for it into the bottom tang and is held closed by a ball bearing on a spring. High pressure gases spray from top and bottom (note the inside of the sling has been blackened by blowby). The Ferguson rifle was nascent technology never developed beyond its original creation. Had it proved tactically successful, the exploration of which was shorted by Ferguson's wounding, the rifle would likely have been perfected. Some later trials showed angling the breechblock forward just a couple of degrees diminished the blast of gas in the face.

Chapter 14
The Brown Bess
Anchor of the Thin Red Line.

THE STANDARD ARM of the Queen's Rangers—and all British infantry—was the Brown Bess, a smoothbore musket averaging .77 caliber that served with only minor changes for more than 100 years beginning in the 1730s. By the late 1840s, the final flintlocks were withdrawn for percussion muskets. All of the Bess muskets are similar in appearance but the myriad models have enough changes in appearance, construction and size to fill a handsome book—and there is one: *The Brown Bess, An Identification and Illustrated Study of Britain's Most Famous Musket,* by Erik Goldstein and Stuart Mowbray. [12]

The Rangers fielded infantry and grenadiers (the big fellows sent to push around smaller opponents) armed with the Brown Bess as the main show. Good for smashing through obstinate lines, grenadiers were the original assault troops. Specialist troops (their own and Hessians) armed with rifles, Royal artillery and cavalry both detached and their own rounded out the whole, but the musket and bayonet in the hands of the infantry and grenadiers is generally how battles were settled. For the chronically undermanned Rangers, the addition of a little chicanery helped, too.

The musket ball added some distance at which infantry could hurl violence

Rangers wore green, but white crossbelts over red coats were the hallmark of the British army for generations along with the solid, dependable Brown Bess musket.

at one another adding noise, a hellishly sulfurous smell along with a heavy pall of smoke over everything. But cold steel still won the battlefield as it had for millennia, and the Brown Bess was more suitable than most (and heavier than most!).

Our example of the Brown Bess is a reproduction made by Pedersoli. Designed to be a generic model similar to ones used in the French & Indian War through the American Revolution, it isn't exactly correct for either period, but good enough for all. It does have the signature features common to the Revolutionary War Brown Bess with a shorter barrel, "handrail" comb and fore-end palm swell. Another constant similarity is Brown Bess smoothbore barrels (especially early ones) weren't always constructed to very exacting tolerances. Barrels can vary considerably and it was only important they weren't too small.

The Pedersoli muskets are built to more exacting tolerances with a .75-inch bore while

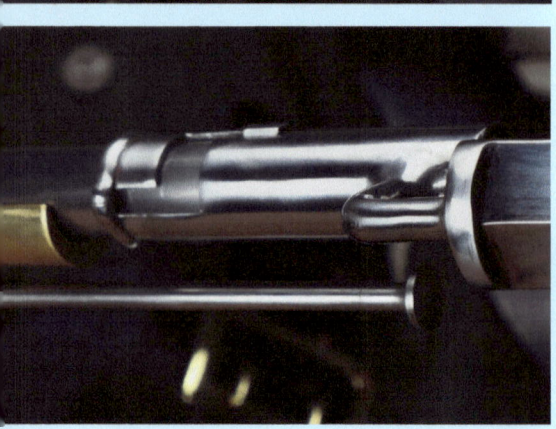

A signal advancement for the infantryman was the adoption of the simple socket bayonet over the plug bayonet around the turn of the 18th century. Plug bayonets often got stuck in the barrel, left in an unfortunate opponent, and if the gun were fired, burst the muzzle. Now the infantryman had a simple way of turning his musket into a stabbing weapon and it was still a shooting weapon. The top of the barrel has a bayonet mounting stud doubling as an aiming post (top) and the bayonet has a zig-zag slot machined at right angles. The bayonet slides over this stud (middle), is turned to the right, and slid back to stop (bottom). Mounted to the side, the bayonet doesn't interfere with loading. A downside not addressed for about a century was if the bayonet was twisted to free it from an unfortunate opponent, it could be pulled free of the arm.

originals could be from .77 to as large as .80. Military ball was originally as small as .690 inch and as large as .715 wrapped in paper. Accuracy by volley fire is understandably sketchy, but the arm stays in the fight and can be loaded and fired quickly for a long time. Initial accuracy may be dismal in a clean musket, but the enemy constantly moves closer and the musket shoots better as it fouls, so combined with the opponent getting closer, the accuracy can improve in a strange (if horrific) way. But the barrel heats up fast becoming uncomfortable after a half dozen rounds.

A smoothbore arm can shoot well if used with properly fitted patch and ball. Many Colonials used a smoothbore for deer hunting with a patched ball (or buckshot) in addition to serving in the militia with paper cartridges.

A sturdily constructed arm, the Bess' long barrel (41¼ inches on the Pedersoli) had metal finished "in the white" (meaning no applied finish at all). It was held to the wooden stock with pins in three places and a screw through the tang. Screws were very expensive and their use held to an absolute minimum. The buttplate, triggerguard and ramrod pipes are of brass, and the rammer of steel. The arm is long at 58½ inches and, when the bayonet is affixed, it is 76¼ inches—taller than most of the men (except maybe the Grenadiers). Heavy at 10 pounds with bayonet affixed, such weight would remain a constant average for military arms until the late 20th century.

These long arms provided effective defense against cavalry (horses won't willingly run into a wall of spikes) as well as infantry. Massed fire created a lot

A signature feature of the Brown Bess for its first 75 years or so was a large palm swell at the point just above the ramrod entry pipe. An aid firing offhand, it allows the shooter to pull the musket more firmly back into the shoulder pocket. Both rifles share this useful feature.

Pulling out the 29-round wooden block reveals a tin tray where spare flints with bits of leather to hold them, tools (like the patch worm) and tow could be stored. An oil bottle fit into one of the cartridge block holes.

of noise and smoke, but commanders on both sides considered a properly handled bayonet the weapon allowing infantry to win battles.

Although they usually had their own rifles, even without them, the Rangers never felt helpless facing American rifles, as has been long been a popular myth in America. This came into play at Spencer's Ordinary (more in Chapter 18), when the Rangers faced off against a wall of Lafayette's riflemen. Simcoe's *Journal* notes, "The principle which Lieut. Col. Simcoe always inculcated and acted on against riflemen, was to rush upon them; when, if each separate company kept itself compact, there was little danger, even should it be surrounded, from troops who were without bayonets, and whose object it was to fire a single shot with effect: the position of an advancing soldier was calculated to lessen the true aim of the first shot, and his rapidity to prevent the rifleman, who requires some time to load, from giving a second; or at least render his aim uncertain, and his fire by no means formidable." [1]

This same technique was used against Continental infantry, too, who often lined up using a rail fence as an impediment. "[T]hey were instructed not to fire, but to charge their bayonets with their muskets loaded, and upon their arrival at the fence, each soldier to take his aim at their opponents, who were then supposed to be driven from it; they were taught that, in the position of running, their bodies afforded a less and more uncertain mark to their antagonists, whose minds also must be perturbed by the rapidity of their approach with undischarged arms." [1] I'll bet! The musket was not noted for accuracy, and volley fire even less so. But charging up on an opponent, then aiming and firing at point blank range would rain such devastation it is not surprising it melted an opposing line.

The Rangers trained further from established doctrine. Simcoe noted on the use of the bayonet, "The grand divisions were exercised in the manual, and firing motions, by their respective commanders, but they were forbidden to teach them to march in slow time, they were, 'to pay great attention to the instruction of their men in charging with their bayonets, in which case, the charge was never to be less than three hundred yards, gradually increasing in celerity from its first outset, taking great care that the grand division has its ranks perfectly close, and the pace adapted to the shortest men. The soldier is, particularly, to be taught, to keep his head well up, and erect: It is graceful on all occasions, but absolutely necessary if an enemy dare stand the charge; when the British soldier, who fixes with his eye the attention of his opponent, and, at the same instant, pushes with his bayonet without looking down on its point, is certain of conquest.'"

Loss of equipment was an issue, too, especially in a light corps detached from the army and far from resupply. An observation by Simcoe paid off when he changed how the infantry approached in line formation, since the first line went forward at advance arms (roughly at an angle looking over the tip of the bayonet) while the rear rank held their arms upright. "[A] number of firelocks were, in action, rendered useless, by being carried on the shoulders, from casual musket-balls which could not be the case were the arms carried in the position of advance." [1]

What's amazing is his idea didn't catch on with the rest of the army.

After a fatal friendly fire incident, Simcoe provided the "Huzzars" with tall shakos with the Ranger's crescent moon and a green toque ending in a tassel. The Potter saber with its distinctive iron guard was their primary weapon.

Rifles, Rangers & Revolution

Chapter 15
Cavalry
Projecting Force by Horse.

MOST LIGHT INFANTRY were just that—infantry. When Simcoe took command of the Queen's Rangers, he quickly saw the need for cavalry. The country was big and his missions would take him far from support of any kind, except for the kindness of loyal strangers. Cavalry would allow him to quickly scout farther and keep apprised of his opponent's movements, as well as providing the muscular support a quick cavalry charge can provide. Obviously, communications with the army via cavalry messengers were far faster than a runner, rising in value the further away from the army the Rangers operated.

Initially, Simcoe was promised detached dragoons for his cavalry, but Simcoe objected, observing, "that the clothing and habiliments of the dragoons were so different from those of the Queen's Rangers (the one wearing the red coat, with white belts, easily seen at a distance, and the Rangers in green, and accoutered for concealment) that he thought it would be more useful to mount a dozen soldiers of the regiment." [1] Lt. General Sir William Erskine agreed and provided horses, saddles and swords.

The Ranger Hussars were dressed in green jackets, with black accoutrements and their green saddle blankets had the crescent moon symbol in the corner. Their tall, black, brimless cylindrical hat was modeled after Hungarian Hussars, and had the crescent moon and a green bag hanging to the side with a white tassel. Green cloth or possibly tan leather trousers and boots rounded out the uniform.

Hussars ("Huzzars" in the Journal) were lightly armed, carrying only a pistol and sword. Hussars were fairly new and modeled after Hungarian light cavalry known for being first in the fight and first out. They also provided a quick shock when necessary and were excellent in a pursuit. Dragoons also composed a portion of the Ranger cavalry. Dragoons carried carbine or musket, pistol and sword, and were meant to ride into an action, then fight on foot—or mounted—making them a versatile force.

Small arms such as pistols and carbines were scarce in the colonies throughout the war, and often only one pistol was issued instead of two, sometimes locally purchased or captured. The heavier musket often replaced the carbine, since carbines were also in very short supply.

The Queen's Rangers were a complete regiment, yet probably eschewed special uniform patterns for the many specialists. The Mounted Rifles (only 12 to start) likely wore their infantry short jacket with ruffled shirt and necktie rather than special dress, but possibly wore Dragoon Tarletons rather than the infantry Mitre hat. The Potter saber would be carried over the shoulder, a belly box would hold a variety of rifle ammunition, a powder measure and a few cartridges for emergency. Just enough gear to accomplish their myriad tasks.

Rifles, Rangers & Revolution

The Queen's Rangers employed "Mounted Rifles, too. Their uniform is not described in the Journal, but were probably accoutered as Dragoons. Simcoe speaks of them as having a rifle (likely a P1776) and sword (likely the Potter saber). Horses would allow fast deployment of their precision fire across the battlefield, and the laying of ambush where fast retreat was essential.

When the Rangers needed more mounted men, whatever British or Hessian units available were detached to them, and the Rangers saw a revolving door of infantry and cavalry units detached for temporary duty to make up the shortfalls or add the specialist troops needed for certain missions.

One unit often serving with the Rangers was Capt. Frederick Diemar's Black Hussars, made up from German prisoners (Brunswickers) who escaped from the Continentals after Burgoyne's defeat. Diemar was originally a captain in the 60th Regiment of Foot (the Royal American Regiment, established during the French & Indian War). Upon a recommendation from Prince Ferdinand of Brunswick, he was given command of the Hussars raised from the idle former prisoners. They worked with Tarleton as well as the Rangers throughout the war, and stayed in North Carolina with the Ranger's Dragoons while Simcoe went with Cornwallis to Yorktown. Diemar would rejoin to the 60th after the peace. [10]

Because they could move so much faster on operations behind enemy lines, cavalry like Hussars were better able to invade, evade and retreat. One episode was rather outrageously audacious involving cavalry as the main thrust. With the approval of Gen. Sir Henry Clinton and Lord Cornwallis, Simcoe volunteered to go far into American territory to find a fleet of 50 flatboats each capable of holding 70 men rumored to have been assembled by General George Washington at Van Vactor's Bridge on the Raritan River for his move on New York. General Washington was awaiting the arrival of the French fleet for a combined action.

Simcoe and his forces moved deep into the Jersies, representing themselves as Continental forces on the lookout for Tories. It worked until someone recognized Simcoe and sent word to New Jersey Governor William Livingston, who raised the alarm.

The Ranger infantry were left to secure the retreat, while the cavalry moved forward into enemy territory. Simcoe found 18 new flatboats full of water sitting on carriages, and got information the others had already been moved. Those boats were destroyed by portfires, hand grenades (each Hussar had been given one) and hatchets. Deep behind enemy lines, opposition began to form behind him. Gen. Mad Anthony Wayne was detached from Washington and marched with light infantry, and Lighthorse Harry Lee was mobilized. Simcoe

Lt. Col. Simcoe led his "Huzzars" deep into the Jersies to destroy boats staged by Washington for an invasion of New York. They carried pistols, hatchets, portfires (not shown) and grenades. The wild escapade was praised by none other than Continental Dragoon Col. Lighthorse Harry Lee (father of Robert E. Lee). The raid was only a partial success, since most of the boats had been moved, and it ended badly when Simcoe was captured. He was later exchanged.

evaded the Continental attempts to intercept him on his way back, but his luck ran out before reaching safety.

After missing a turning, Simcoe's guide inadvertently led him directly into an ambush where Continentals fired their muskets at point blank range as Simcoe rode by. His horse, struck by five shots was killed, he was thrown and knocked unconscious by the fall. Simcoe awoke captured. Thinking him dead, his cavalry retreated to safety after a brief skirmish. He was nearly murdered by militia angry over their losses during the skirmish, but saved by cooler heads. Governor Livingston was angry enough about the incident to give Simcoe a written protection.

Lighthorse Harry Lee mentions the end of this episode in his Memoirs, recalling, "This enterprise [destroying the boats] was considered by both armies, among the handsomest exploits of the war. Simcoe executed completely his object, then deemed very important; and traversed the country, from Elizabethtown Point to South Amboy, fifty-five miles, in the course of the night and morning; passing through a most hostile region of armed citizens; necessarily skirting Brunswick, a military station; proceeding not more than eight or nine miles from the legion of Lee, his last point of danger, and which increased from the debilitated condition to which his troops were reduced by previous fatigue.

"What is very extraordinary, Lt. Col. Simcoe, being obliged to feed once in the course of the night, stopped at a depot of forage collected for the Continental army, assumed the character of Lee's cavalry, waked up the commissary about midnight, drew the customary allowance of forage, and gave the usual vouchers, signing the name of legion Quartermaster, without being discovered by the American forage commissary, or his assistants. The dress of both corps was the same, green coatees and leather breeches; yet the success of the stratagem is astonishing." [1]

Lighthorse Harry Lee corresponded with Simcoe during his imprisonment until Simcoe was exchanged a few months later to rejoin the Rangers.

Rifles, Rangers & Revolution

Chapter 16
Arms of the Cavalry
Sabres, rifles, carbines, pistols.

THE PRIMARY MOUNTED weapon was the saber, and the most-issued one was the New York-made Potter Light Dragoon sabers, manufactured by loyalist James Potter. Of the 1,580 swords purchased for British use, 349 are listed in the records as being for provincial forces such as the Queen's Rangers. James Potter's swords earned a solid reputation for quality, and were coveted by Colonial cavalry. Based on the British Pattern 1756 Light Dragoon saber, the Potter had a similar curved slashing blade having a length of about 35 to 37 inches (plenty of variation exists, and many were shortened in their service life) with a unique squared and pierced iron hilt carried in a leather sheath. The sheath had a button to fit a frog, an iron throat, iron chape and was worn over the shoulder on a belt in the same way as the bayonet.

Potter is known to have had a forger and two or three filers working for him, but it is not likely he forged the blades in New York. Industrialization was in its infancy here, and surviving blades are of good, consistent quality, so it is probable blades were imported from Britain, or even Germany. The address of his New York shop was in an area without a waterworks to power a forge and trip hammers to make the blades, although they could have been run by a horse gin. You'd think if it was a fully set up iron works, there would be some record of it after Potter quit New York. Potter delivered all those swords to the British in three years between 1779 and 1781. [17] Hard to imagine such a small group could forge them from ore to blade in such quantities.

Potter swords were issued to all units raised in America and many that came over. Tarleton's British Legion Dragoons were the most famous to use them, along with the Hussars and Dragoons of the Queen's Rangers.

Among the Colonials, Light Horse Harry Lee's Dragoons carried Potter swords. Supplying them was not as easy as a task as you'd imagine, since the Colonial cavalry had to use captured ones, and they were considered quite a prize. The Continentals sent a captured one to James Hunter's iron works on the Rappahannock River in Virginia to copy. Maj. Richard Call of the 3rd

The Eliott Light Dragoon pistol was the only firearm Hussars carried (when they could get them). "Huzzars" as Simcoe called them, were used for scouting and rapid communications, but their singular fast strike ability in battle was their key asset.

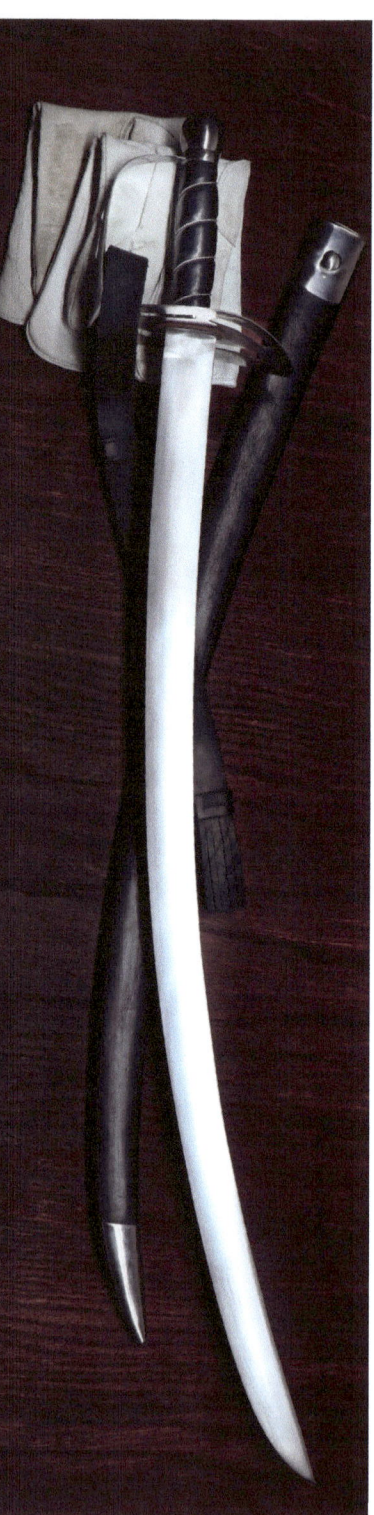

Light Dragoons wrote Virginia's Governor Thomas Jefferson, "I have received Express from Lt. Col. Washington one Horseman's sword taken in the late action at Guilford Court House, which he directs me to send Mr. Hunter as a pattern and have swords made for the men." Call adds, "…the sword is most destructive and almost only necessary weapon a Dragoon carries." [17] This happened late enough in the war the Patriots wouldn't be able to field the 1,000 swords from Hunter until after hostilities were mostly over.

Potter was a loyalist through and through and didn't wait to see what fate might befall him after the Battle of Yorktown. Potter sold out, packed up and resettled in Nova Scotia. And there James Potter fades from history, leaving behind a sword unique to the American Revolution.

While the sword was the favored weapon of mounted men, they carried pistols, too. But pistols were scarce, and could have been of the old heavy Dragoon pattern or the newer, smaller Eliott Light Dragoon pistol as well as captured French or Spanish pistols. The Eliott became the official pistol in the 1760s. No sights, it is meant for the contact range fights between cavalrymen.

Smoothbore carbines firing the lighter .62 caliber ball (same as the rifle) were shorter in length, lighter in weight and carried on a wider shoulder strap with a snap hook attached to a sling-ring on a long bar on the gun rather than slung across the back with a conventional sling. Carbines were also always in short supply, and proved fragile in service due to being more lightly built than the heavier .77-caliber Brown Bess musket. Often substituted, especially with Dragoons, the Bess had to be slung muzzle up to keep the rammer in place, a solid advantage for the P1776 with its captured rammer.

The James Potter saber was relatively light in weight at 2½ pounds with a wooden grip covered in leather and wrapped with twisted wire. The iron guard is pierced in four places and makes a sharp bend. The curved, slashing blade is smooth with no fuller, and tapers through its modest blade length of 35 or so inches. Its false edge runs about 7 inches along the top.

Rifles, Rangers & Revolution

Chapter 17
The Chicanery Of Action
Always Practice to Deceive.

THE RANGERS OFTEN operated far from help. On such missions, Simcoe made up for his lack of superior force with imagination and a bit of magic, and was a master of deception making his small, understrength force appear larger than it was.

Early in June, 1781, Cornwallis ordered the Rangers on a quiet move toward American Gen. Baron Friedrich von Steuben and his presumed 300 or 400 men who had made a river crossing at the fork of the James River, Virginia, with a great deal of stores. The Rangers were sorely depleted, down to about 200 infantry and 100 cavalry. Of those men, who had been working far from resupply, many had worn out their shoes to the point nearly 50 men were essentially barefoot. Many of their uniforms were in sad shape as well. Simcoe gave the men without shoes the choice to stay behind, but none did.

Cornwallis detached 200 red coats of the 71st and a 3-pounder "Grasshopper" battery to bulk up the Ranger force. The Rangers were able to move close without Baron Steuben becoming aware. Not a bad trick, since "red coats" were a dead giveaway, but the use of an advanced cavalry screen was the key. Lt. Spencer and 20 chosen Hussars on the "fleetest horses" formed the advanced guard. Anyone in sight was detained, and no alarm raised of the Ranger's approach.

The infantry advanced in two battalions, alternating who was in front. If attacked, the first battalion was to form a line, and the second a column ready to march to either flank. Over the 2-day march, as prisoners and intelligence were gathered, the force approached Napier's ford at the junction of the North and South Forks of the James. Simcoe found Baron von Steuben's force was 900 men—more than double the force predicted—and more militia were on the way. Freshly unloaded from Continental boats, arms and stores were visible on the banks.

The goal now was to make von Steuben think the small force of Rangers were the advance of Cornwallis' whole army closing on him. Here, having red coats along proved valuable, since by now it was well known the Rangers wore green. The 71st, in the red coats, were ordered to assemble on the banks of the river within sight of the Americans across the river, but not close enough to be fired upon. To improve the deception, Simcoe had his baggage train with the women halt in the woods on the summit of the hill, where they were just visible and thus gave "the appearance of a numerous corps."

A 3-pounder was "carried down" (one of the few instances where the ease of movement over difficult terrain these lightweight guns had is chronicled) to the banks and ordered the Artillerymen to take the best aim possible and fire one shot. Their shot killed the horse of one of Baron von Steuben's orderly dragoons. Now Steuben knew artillery was present, usually the harbinger of a larger force assembling.

Welcome Bounty!

Night fell without action, and by the sounds, it was deduced von Steuben was destroying the boats used in the crossing. Still, fearing a nighttime counterattack, Simcoe's men slept under arms, and the cavalry maintained patrols. But daylight found von Steuben gone, leaving the stores behind. Five "huzzars" were sent across the river with their saddles to catch horses left behind by von Steuben. They were to mount and, if encountering an enemy patrol, "to make a great shout and every demonstration of pursuing them, to impress them with the idea that the whole corps had passed." When the Huzzars encountered Continental cavalry sent back for intelligence, their patrol, "upon perceiving them, fled with utmost speed."

It was later learned Baron von Steuben, upon receiving the report of this patrol, moved another 20 miles on top of the 30 miles already marched from the fork. The Baron must have believed the whole of Cornwallis' army was nearly upon him, since he left behind 2,500 stands of arms, numerous French cannons and mortars still in working order. Usually—even under intense pressure—Gunners will spike all the cannon by driving a nail into the touchhole before retreat to render them unusable against the retreating force.

Also abandoned in their haste were many kegs of gunpowder, some 60 hogsheads of rum, brandy, and sundry other supplies. What the Rangers couldn't take with them, they destroyed. I suspect some had a merry time of it!

Rifles, Rangers & Revolution

Chapter 18
Spencer's Ordinary
The Master of Chicanery at work again!

IN ONE OF their last actions, on 26 June, 1781, Simcoe played another Grand Illusion just north of Williamsburg, Virginia. A small contingent of 300 Queen's Rangers (including cavalry and 3-pounder Grasshoppers) held off a larger force estimated at 1,200 men sent by Marquis de Lafayette, and led by Col. Richard Butler. Just a few days earlier, Cornwallis gave Simcoe orders to march toward Chickahominy to search out a foundry and some boats. He was to destroy them, and collect all the cattle he could. Cornwallis warned Simcoe he would be operating 2 or 3 days behind the army, but the army should meet him at Williamsburg.

Finding no foundry or boats, the Rangers collected the cattle, much to the dismay of the farmers, no doubt (so much for "hearts and minds"). Simcoe knew Lafayette was in the area, and that he may have been, or soon would be joined by Gen. "Mad" Anthony Wayne. The Colonial goal was understood to be, "to take any little advantage which they could magnify in their newspapers." With no reliable intelligence, Simcoe promised a man he knew to be a rebel a great reward if he could find Lafayette, asking he be certain to return the next morning at which time the Rangers would march. Simcoe then sent his cannon, infantry and Jägers to Spencer's Ordinary, about 7 miles north of Williamsburg at 2 a.m. Spencer's Ordinary (a common name for a tavern in those days) sits at the fork of the road leading south to Jamestown and Williamsburg. The collected cattle were sent on their way to Cornwallis with the baggage wagons.

Simcoe planned to engage the Continentals at Spencer's Ordinary long enough for the cattle to be moved. Upon arriving at the Ordinary, Simcoe observed the ground and remarked to his officers, "That it was an admirable place for the chicanery of action." Simcoe ordered the fences thrown down, for his cavalry to feed their horses at nearby Lee's farm, and picketed the Highlanders in the wood.

The appearance of Continental cavalry caused a skirmish. The Ranger cavalry charged from Lee's farm and broke the American flank, scattering them. Many were dismounted, but before all could be captured, a heavy fire from the advance American riflemen broke out in the wood, driving out the

Highlanders. The Continental prisoners taken confirmed Lafayette and Generals Wayne and Steuben were at "no great distance."

Simcoe directed his infantry to form in three groups spread at wide intervals to cover the great span of ground between the road to Jamestown on their left and a wood on their right. Infantry was on the left, Grenadiers and Light Infantry in the center, and Capt. Johann von Ewald and the rifles of his Hesse-Kassel Jägers on the right. Simcoe situated his mounted rifles under Capt. Althuse where they could check any sally by the Continentals from the woods.

The plan was to outflank the enemy by the length of the line. Simcoe judged the line of riflemen he was facing were part of Lafayette's advance corps. The technique would be to rush the riflemen, thus disturbing their aim and make them rush their reload. Their lack of bayonets would be met by a volley and bayonet charge.

Simcoe had ordered the baggage wagons toward Williamsburg with the cattle, and had instructed those men to cut down trees and barricade the first pass where the Rangers could rally. Simcoe then moved with the cavalry out of sight of the Continentals, down a hill, ascending again at Lee's farm. There the entire cavalry force (such as it was) paraded in front of the Continentals, then fell back behind the hill leaving a detachment of "Huzzars" to keep the illusion of a greater force alive. They would prevent the left from being turned and hopefully deceive the Continentals in the belief all the cavalry (whom they had already engaged once) were waiting for the opportunity to strike.

Simcoe's deception centered on making the Continentals believe he had a far larger body of men than he did. He deployed his 3-pounder Grasshoppers, cavalry and infantry in such a fashion they appeared to be supported by a larger force behind a hill to his rear, but, of course, he had no such reserves.

The Continentals now approached in force, lining the fences on the edge of the wood in front of the infantry, refusing their right upon reaching open ground in belief the whole Ranger cavalry was lurking (as Simcoe hoped). Simcoe ordered one cannon shot be fired at the body of infantry at the greatest

"Throwing Down the Fences at Spencer's Ordinary." His force small at around 300, and separated from Gen. Cornwallis by at least a day, Lt. Col. Simcoe prepared to meet Lafayette's advance force with the "chicanery of action." Some fences at Spencer's were thrown down so the Continentals wouldn't use them as a barrier against an infantry charge, and the battery of 3-pounder cannon placed to cover the battlefield, yet in such a position the Continentals wouldn't be sure reserves weren't right behind.

distance. The Ranger infantry now advanced as fast as the fields would allow.

Simcoe expected no victory—his goal was to buy the cattle and baggage convoy time to reach Cornwallis, then gain the wood and make a retreat to the rally point.

The Continentals tried to flank the approaching British infantry, and Simcoe's secreted cavalry surprised and dispersed them. Ranger Lt. Charles Dunlop, who had been with the Corps since age 13, advanced his infantry, giving them a signal to lay down whenever the opposition leveled their arms to fire. "He arrived at the fence where the enemy had been posted with his arms loaded, a conduct that might have been decisive of the action." [1] Dunlop did not lose a man to enemy fire, but the Continentals could not say the same. Nothing like a point-blank volley at the point of the bayonet to break a line! Capt. Ewald and his rifle-armed Jägers turned the Continental left flank and "gave them a severe fire as they fled in utmost confusion." Ewald had wanted the support of bayonet men, and had he had them, likely would have caused much more grief to the Continentals. There were of course, no reserves.

To Simcoe's surprise, the enemy now bought the idea they were facing a larger force, and perhaps Cornwallis himself, and withdrew. The Rangers lost 10 men and had 23 wounded, and the Jägers 1 killed and 2 wounded. The Rangers took 32 prisoners, many of them officers and from many different corps. Fearing the Continentals would reform and advance, Simcoe ordered a retreat. With no wagons, he left his wounded and dead at Spencer's Ordinary with a surgeon and a flag of truce while he moved to find Gen. Cornwallis.

His deception was a total success. When a Continental patrol mistook a foraging party from Cornwallis along the Williamsburg Road for the advance guard of the army, the Continentals retreated in panic and confusion. Lt. Col. Tarleton and his Dragoons advanced up the road soon after and found a great number of arms thrown away and other signs of a hasty Continental retreat. Simcoe returned to Spencer's Ordinary and was able to retrieve his wounded, his surgeon and his dead. One of the dead was the formerly mentioned Sgt. M'Pherson, killed while charging the Continental right flank with the mounted riflemen under Capt. Shank.

Putting on a good face, Lafayette noted in a letter to Virginia's governor, "Colonel Simcoe was so lucky as to avoid a part of the stroke; but, although the whole of the light corps could not arrive in time, some of them did. Major MacPherson having taken up fifty light infantry behind fifty dragoons, overtook Simcoe, and, regardless of numbers, made an immediate charge. He was supported by the riflemen, who behaved most gallantly and did great

Rifles, Rangers & Revolution

execution. The alarm-guns were fired at Williamsburg (only six miles distant from the field.) A detachment then going to Gloucester was recalled, and the whole British army came out to save Simcoe. They retired next morning, when our army got within striking distance.

"Our loss is two captains, ten privates wounded; two lieutenants, one sergeant, six privates killed; one lieutenant, twelve privates, whose fate is not known; one sergeant taken. The enemy had about sixty killed, among whom are several officers, and about one hundred wounded. They acknowledge the action was smart, and Lord Cornwallis was heard to express himself vehemently upon the disproportion between his and our killed, which must be attributed to the great skill of our riflemen." [1] While Simcoe's losses appear highly exaggerated by Lafayette, it also appears Simcoe's "chicanery of action" worked its magic.

With so few men against more than 1,200 Continentals, Simcoe was justifiably proud of each and every man. As related in his *Journal*, "…Lt. Col. Simcoe has ever considered this action as the climax of a campaign of five years, as the result of true discipline acquired in that space by unremitted diligence, toil, and danger, as an honourable victory earned by veteran intrepidity."

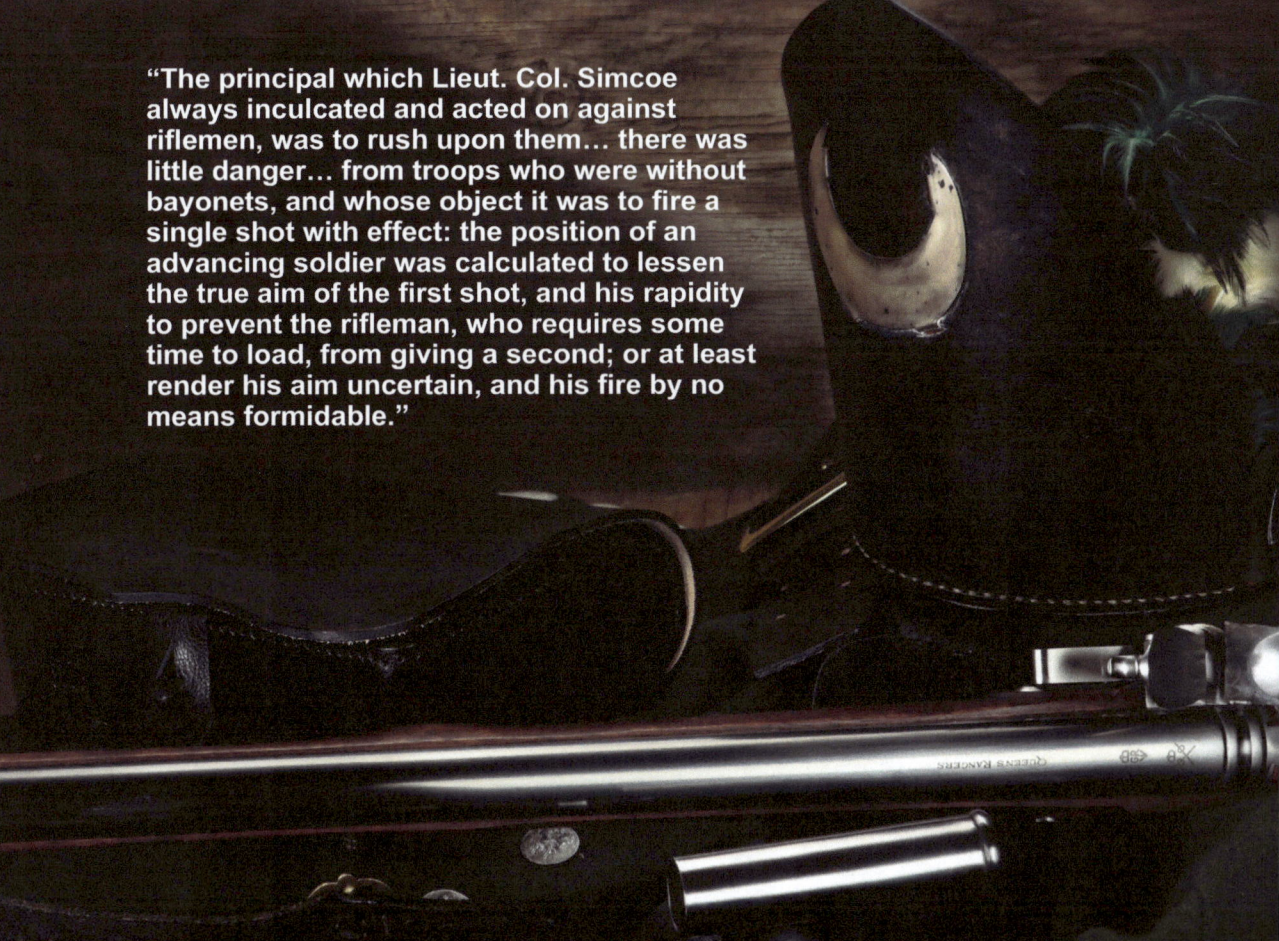

"The principal which Lieut. Col. Simcoe always inculcated and acted on against riflemen, was to rush upon them… there was little danger… from troops who were without bayonets, and whose object it was to fire a single shot with effect: the position of an advancing soldier was calculated to lessen the true aim of the first shot, and his rapidity to prevent the rifleman, who requires some time to load, from giving a second; or at least render his aim uncertain, and his fire by no means formidable."

Part III
Chapter 19
The Grasshopper Gun
A purpose-built cannon for America.

THE RANGERS USED every tool at Spencer's Ordinary: infantry, cavalry, riflemen, mounted rifles and artillery in the form of a pair of 3-pounder guns. These marvelous little 3-pounder "Grasshopper" and "Butterfly" guns used so successfully in the American Revolution were completely new cannon from the ground up, designed expressly for use in America, and brought economy along with utility to the new warfare in the Colonies. All the 80+ 3-pounders—Pattison, Townsend and Congreve—were cast, finished and proofed by August of 1776.

The concept of lightweight guns was born of continental developments during the Seven Years' War (French & Indian War in America). Frederick the Great's Prussian army successfully used new tactics for his lightweight 3- and 6-pounder guns moving easily and rapidly across the battlefield to give support to the infantry as conditions and positions changed. Frederick the Great could quickly move his light guns where they were needed most, while his opponents used traditional tactics keeping their artillery (which consisted of big, heavy, hard-to-move guns) in one place. Mobility had arrived.

Observing their effect, Col. James Pattison of the Royal Artillery opined a light 3-pounder gun would be ideal for use in the colonies, and set about designing a gun not only lightweight, but with a carriage that could be pulled by one horse, carried intact by eight men, broken down and packed on two horses or carried in pieces by 16 men when the vestigial roads of the New World turned to trails, then deer tracks as inevitably happened. Promoted to Major General, Pattison would come to America and be in charge of artillery during the Revolution from 1777 to 1780.

A 1773 document laying out the principals of this new gun compares its effectiveness to the 6-pounder noting, "That a 3 pounder Round Shot it is apprehended is capable of every mischievous effect that can be wished against Troops in the Field." [11]

Pattison's design would see fruition not only as a clever gun carriage, but in the barrel design itself as a short, lightweight bronze tube made to perfection by new manufacturing techniques. In conjunction with this new design, big changes were instituted by the Board of Ordnance to modernize the rundown Woolwich Arsenal, where the Crown's cannon had long been founded. They were made pretty much the way cannon had been made for hundreds of years. Not only was output low and rejection rate high, but the technology in place was long obsolete and in complete disrepair. Britain had been at the fore of new founding and cannon finishing technology in the late 1600s (see Appendix iv), but let it die for a variety of reasons.

The new master founder brought new technology and new ideas to the fore, and made possible a substantially increased output of high-quality tubes ensuring a steady flow of artillery for the conflict. The methods devised by Woolwich for bronze cannon were adapted for the Royal Navy's iron cannon, and (not surprisingly) coincides with the technology making Watt's steam engine possible (see Appendix iv again).

The 3-pounder "Grasshopper" guns were light and mobile, allowing the Queen's Rangers to appear more formidable than they were. Such chicanery became a hallmark of the Rangers.

Chapter 20
A Modern Era
Let the Industrial Revolution begin!

BRITISH ARTILLERY WAS in a sorry state in 1769 with the arsenal's foundry run down, out of date and in overall poor repair with little output. One of the best foundrymen in the world was Dutchman Jan Verbruggen. He and his son Pieter were hired away from Holland's bell and cannon foundry at Enkhuizen in 1770 to modernize the entire cannon manufacturing process for the British. It wasn't a difficult choice for Verbruggen, since he had made bitter enemies in Holland, ones determined to ruin him and trample his reputation. It is a wonder the Board of Ordnance took a chance on him, but it proved wise. Construction of a new foundry at Woolwich and other improvements began immediately by the Verbruggens. By 1773, England was ready to turn out state-of-the-art cannon barrels.

Verbruggen improved on the processes he used in Holland, ones credited to Swiss-born Jean Maritz who had been founding and boring high-quality cannon for the Swiss since 1715. While Maritz's sons took the processes to France and Spain in the mid 1750s, England had stayed with the old processes. Maritz may not have been the originator of the process, but he certainly improved it (see Appendix iv).

What made the Maritz/Verbruggen style of barrel manufacturing so much better (and Wilkinson's in iron) was the cannon barrel was founded as one solid piece instead of casting them around a core inside the mold nominally of the bore size. These "newel bars" used to form the bores often warped or failed, leaving the bore difficult to ream, since the bit followed the path cast into the tube. It was not unusual for such barrels to have other flaws in the casting, too.

When the tube was poured around a newel bar, the breech end often wound up having casting flaws of some nature. Such cannon were more prone to bursting unpredictably. Another serious problem was a misaligned bore. Bore-to-sight alignment problems were common with such cannons. If bored off center even a little, they wouldn't shoot anywhere near where they were pointed, especially as range increased. The gunner had to know his gun, since it could shoot anywhere but where it was pointed!

Casting the barrel as a solid piece, then boring to caliber on the horizontal lathe was a significant improvement to accuracy, repeatability and strength. Casting these tubes solid in vertical molds, Verbruggen's cannon were stronger

Woolwich Arsenal's furnace could pour 38,000 pounds of molten bronze at one time. The speed of the pour was controlled by the gent manipulating the long rod at the end of the pit. The cannon molds were buried muzzle up in the pit, and filled sequentially. It is thought the white haired gentleman is Jan Verbruggen. Foundry Drawing 39 by Jan Verbruggen courtesy the van Doesburgh Foundation.

at the breech end due to the pressure caused by metal compressing under the weight of the entire pour minimizing air bubbles and casting inclusions. Boring to caliber from solid allowed very careful adherence to caliber tolerances and allowed for a finely finished bore improving both accuracy and ease of cleaning.

Verbruggen added lathe turning of the outside while boring the inside allowing him to control internal and external dimensions far more closely. The lathe-turned outside wound up creating another benefit by revealing any flaws in the casting on the surface. The casting in place of decorative or heraldic designs long a fixture of cannon tubes slowly disappear since it slowed production. The little 3-pounder tubes, among the first cast, had no decorations and markings were handstamped.

While a finished 3-pounder tube weighed only 200 pounds or so, this giant apparatus was able to revolve the heavy (almost 4-ton) 42-pounder gun against the fixed bit. The maximum speed this lathe reached was only between 7 and 4½ rpm. Power was supplied by a 4-horse gin, and cannon tube manufacture during the war increased to the point Verbruggen had to ask the Board of Ordnance for an allowance for four more horses and enough fodder to keep them going. Horses were given 10-minutes rest every hour. Woolwich Arsenal used the horse gin until the 1840s when horses were finally replaced with steam power.

The bronze (usually called brass in the day) in these barrels was composed of 90 percent copper and 10 percent tin. The furnace was capable of melting 17 long tons of metal (38,080 pounds) at a time, and the master founder responsible for keeping the proportions right. An art in those days, since even when smelting old barrels, the original tin burned off and had to be added.

While bronze was heavier than iron, bronze barrels could be made lighter since they were stronger. Add that bronze was more corrosion resistant, would rupture rather than burst like a bomb as did iron, and could be recycled at the end of its service life (unlike iron which had to be scrapped). The choice of material was an obviously good one, if far more expensive initially. It is also why the survival rate of bronze guns is low, since the material remains very useful in war.

The Verbruggen's reworking of Woolwich Arsenal may best be judged by the increased output and the number of barrels passing proof. During the Seven Years War from 1756-63, 27.2% of the previous master founder's 187 tubes were rejected. During the American Revolution, the Verbruggens submitted 578 tubes for proof with a rejection rate of only 2.6%. [16]

Verbruggen's modernization of Woolwich Arsenal included casting the barrel solid, boring to caliber on a lathe against a fixed bit while turning the outside smooth. Foundry Drawing 47 by Jan Verbruggen courtesy the van Doesburgh Foundation.

Chapter 21
Three 3-pounders
There was surprising variety in the little guns.

AMONG THE FIRST of these new high-quality cannon tubes cast by Verbruggen were for Pattison's light 3-pounder gun fitted to the carriage soon to be nicknamed the "Grasshopper." Six were cast in 1775 and sent to America (three survive today). Either four or eight of a second, slightly lighter barrel designed by Mr. Ward, Surveyor General of the Ordnance in Ireland, and submitted by Master General of the Ordnance Lord Townshend were cast, with the idea the gun could be more easily carried (they are called "Townshends, and at least one survives).

The third one, a barrel and new carriage designed by Captain William Congreve, Royal Artillery, was the final barrel design, and the one cast in the greatest numbers and seeing the most service. They began arriving on the shores of America in 1776. All three barrel designs were similar in weight and length, but are different enough they can be readily identified by sight, scale and measure. (Capt. Congreve went on to develop the Congreve rocket that figures so prominently in the United States' National anthem *The Star Spangled Banner* written during the War of 1812.)

Seventy-two Congreve guns crossed the sea for service in America (and about 14 tubes survive). Congreve carriages (nicknamed Butterflies) didn't have the brackets for hand carry like the Grasshopper and were provided with three ammunition chests. Two smaller ammunition chests fitted over the axle on either side of the barrel, and the third longer one in the trail.

Whether Grasshopper or Butterfly, a 3-pounder pulled alone by a single horse was called a "Galloper" with no limber attached. When attached to a limber, there was room for much more of the gunner's gear necessary to run the gun. As envisioned, the limber for the Congreve is unique, in that it contained rawhide shields called "mantlets" that could be deployed to protect the gun team from small arms fire. On a battery of two guns, these mantlets also mounted two "wall guns"—enlarged Land Pattern muskets having 1-inch bores—for defense of the gunners. I've encountered no evidence these little guns were ever used as envisioned. Sometimes the best laid plan goes awry. But the technique of the unfolding mantlets have left us with a colorful nickname for the little gun.

The limber would be needed to transport the two extra ammo boxes when used with the Grasshopper carriage, since the brackets for hand carry precluded placing the twin boxes over the axle. When two horses were required, they were hitched in tandem rather than side-by-side. Extra ammunition could follow in an ammunition tumbril (a small, two-wheeled cart).

These little 3-pounders were versatile guns, even if all the imaginative ideas concerning their transport, use and defense never quite made it into action. The simple fact they could be hauled up and down steep slopes by men or horses made them very useful in the Americas, especially during coastal or frontier operations where heavier guns would be difficult to move.

The presence of artillery caused opponents to consider their next moves more carefully. Cannon usually implied a bigger force, and the Rangers used the illusion to their advantage often. The little 3-pounder guns were more mobile and easier to use than more powerful guns, but could be more bother than they were worth. Lt. Col. Simcoe left them behind on occasion when Royal Artillerymen weren't available to man them, and Continental commander Francis Marion, the "Swamp Fox" himself, pushed two them into a swamp when pressed hard, and never bothered himself with cannon again.

Chapter 22
Puzzles & Power
Small gun, small punch.

NONE OF THE many stories about the nickname "Grasshopper" can be proven, but all are fun and plausible. One is the gun hops off the ground under recoil, which many guns do. Another is the way it bounced around as it was galloped across the field into position. The best story is it looks like a grasshopper with the hand spikes installed fore-and-aft for "Irish carry." Maybe all three. Artillerists are famous for nicknaming guns.

Pattison, Townsend or Congreve, a 3-pound gun was never the big game changer for the grand battles generals planned. The most useful cannon of the day was the 6-pounder gun, and it remained so in America until just before the Civil War. But the small 3-pounder guns weighed little, and required fewer resources to build, transport, support and man. They were easier to land ashore, and could be hauled up cliff sides by ropes far easier than the bigger Battalion guns.

As well as being maneuverable in the wilds and around the battlefield, a lot more of them could make a trip overseas, and they were easier for small units to manage. The limbers and carriages were fabricated in America and only the tubes had to be shipped.

The records indicate some iron 3-pounder barrels were cast. There is no record any of them saw battle, and it is supposed they were sent over as patterns for the artillery carriage makers to use. There is no record of how many Grasshopper and Butterfly carriages were made, but the tubes would fit either one, and a gun could be outfitted with the most practicable carriage for the desired needs of a mission at the artillery park.

That the ammunition load was more manageable was evidently a selling point, too, since a battle load of ammunition could go on the gun, not as part of a separate baggage t rain or tumbril. "It is well known to all Officers who have served Campaigns abroad how difficult it is for the Light 6 Pounder Battalion Guns to keep up on ordinary marches… and how much more so on any March which requires extra-ordinary Expedition, especially as the Waggons which carry their Ammunition are constructed on such false Principles as to render it impracticable for them to travel with any degree of Speed, even in the Best weather and in common roads, but absolutely impossible… when the roads are naturally in their worse state." [11]

Chapter 23
Pounds & Power
Less can be more.

WHERE THE LITTLE 3-pounder guns fell short was in battering fortifications. Fortuitously, America had few to batter, and those were often of wood. Against a farmhouse it was a titan. Against a timber fort, not so much. Against infantry and cavalry, it was deadly. Maximum range of the little gun was around 800 to 1,000 yards (including skips) at 3 degrees, 30 minutes elevation, so these were up close and personal guns. That they could be moved quickly was a plus.

While greater elevation could launch the shot farther, doing so caused the ball to plunge into the earth. Firing at the lesser elevations caused the 2.77-inch 3-pound iron ball to ricochet and skip along the ground. The more unpredictable the bounce, the more the opposition's lines could be broken if not by actual casualties as the ball plowed through men or horses, then by causing the men to do the cannon ball hop as it passed. Cannon balls were exceptionally dangerous until they *stopped* rolling, as many found to their regret by getting a broken foot trying to stop one slowly rolling toward them.

Because the elevation of the muzzle was so slight, power and range could be controlled through the charge itself. Grasshoppers used a variety of charges from ½ to full in bags filled ahead of time by the Artillerymen. The charge weight was painted on the end in ounces.

As the opposition moved in, the little 3-pounders guns presented the nasty surprise of case shot, a tin can holding a 36 musket balls (about 2½ pounds). While the maximum range was about 350 yards, it was far more devastating at the close ranges of 100 or 150.

By then the artillerymen had to think about scooting. This meant hitching up the guns (assuming counter battery fire hadn't wiped out the horse). If overrun, always a concern with any gun, artillerists had to make sure the guns were either spiked by driving a large nail into the touchhole, or remove enough implements the guns couldn't be turned on their men as they retreated. Guns were often traded back and forth this way several times.

In defensive situations, some imagination helped make artillery more effective. Outposted to Richmond on Staten Island, New York, in the winter of 1780, Lt. Col. Simcoe's Queen's Rangers and Captain Frederick de Diemer of the Black Hussars (attached) were given the area considered "the most remote and most susceptible to surprise and capture." [10] As usual, the Queen's Rangers were understrength and Simcoe had to improvise to give his force the ability to withstand attack by a larger one.

The redoubts were fortified and traps were set to funnel the attack where Simcoe could muster the greatest firepower. Simcoe inherited a 9- and two 6-pound guns on platforms. These were "without embrasures, in the redoubts: these were pointed at the eminences, where it was expected the enemy would first appear, and where stones were collected in heaps, so that a round shot, if it struck among them, might have the effect of grape." [1] Such an inventive act likely means there was little or no canister or grape left with the guns. "Without embrasures" meant they were in a far less defensible a position than desirable.

These cannon weren't expendable, but if the Continentals brought up cannon, Simcoe planned to abandon the right redoubt on their appearance, fill its area with prepared abatis, then leave open its gate exposing it to the fire of his two regimental field pieces (Grasshoppers, no doubt, but not specified). They would be supported with musketry from the doors, windows and loop holes in the barracks.

One of the traps meant to influence the path the enemy took was a nasty one. Nails were driven through boards and the boards placed under the snow along the likely approaches. An attack never materialized. Deserters reported Continental officers felt, "'That it was not worthwhile to attack Richmond where they were sure of obstinate resistance, and which must fall of itself whenever the main body was taken.'" [1] The Continentals withdrew.

Chapter 24
Bait & Switch
The Osborne's.

OFFENSIVELY, A LITTLE imagination helped increase the value of the Grasshoppers, and there was none better at using the assets available to him to their utmost than General Benedict Arnold. Once one of the Continental Army's most intrepid soldiers, Arnold switched sides in 1780, becoming a Brigadier General for the British serving under Major General William Phillips. The Queen's Rangers along with the 80th and 76th regiments were put under Arnold's command. Before departing New York, a wary Gen. Clinton, gave "dominant commissions" to Cols. Dundas and Simcoe, two men he trusted utterly, "authorising them, if they suspect Arnold of sinister intent, to supersede him, and put him in arrest." [1]

Arnold proved faithful, and proceeded south with his men and artillery to the Osborne's near Richmond in Virginia, to molest the Navy of the Commonwealth of Virginia. There, Arnold found six ships, eight brigs, five sloops, two schooners, and a number of smaller craft. The chief vessels were Tempest, 20 guns; Renown, 16; and Jefferson, 14. Many of the rest were loaded with the currency of Virginia—tobacco—among other useful stores. These warships had been commissioned to defend Virginia from the predations of the British, who had effectively secured the states to the south. Manning and equipping them was problematic for the Commonwealth, but they did what they could.

On April 27, 1781, Arnold encountered these ships quietly anchored. All were still undermanned, with the recruiting of sailors and Marines proving slow (not that they could provide a full compliment of arms for the Marines anyway, and some of these ships had no arms). Although it was well known

Masters of the "chicanery of war" were Brigadier General Benedict Arnold and Lt. Col. Simcoe. At the Osbornes in Virginia (left), Arnold placed his 3-pounders to annoy the 20-gun Virginia State ship Tempest at anchor. Their fire, which was doing little harm, coaxed Tempest into turning her broadside towards them. Tempest was rewarded with a raking fire through her stern from Arnold's concealed battery of 6 pounders. Supporting fire by other ships cut an anchor cable setting Tempest adrift. Since both Simcoe and Arnold were careful with the lives of their men, it's likely the "bait" were told to take cover when fired upon! Art: Jeff John

Phillips and Arnold were moving through Virginia and a detachment had already destroyed the shipyard, including vessels and warehouses at Chickahominy just five days earlier, Arnold took care in this march to remain undiscovered and enjoyed complete surprise. No information of his force reached the ships until Arnold approached under a flag of truce. Arnold asked the Commodore of the little fleet to surrender with an offer to allow them to keep half their cargo. With spirit, the Commander responded he was determined to "defend it to the last extremity."

The 20-gun Virginia State ship Tempest sat before Arnold anchored at the bow and stern with spring cables. Ships so anchored can be turned mechanically without need of wind so their full broadside can be brought to bear on any angle of attack from sea or land. Arnold brought up his two 3-pounders to fire on her, and she swung her broadside upon the little guns. [1, 13]

Duck!

Nothing is recorded about whether the artillerists manning the 3-pounders were read in on the joke of being set up as ninepins for a broadside, but it is hoped they were instructed to duck. The Tempest had little to fear from the two 3-pounders, but cannon fire is cannon fire, and it is not sensible to just sit there and take it if you can offer a rebuke. However, in swinging around to engage them, Tempest exposed her stern to another part of the shore.

Luckily for the plucky little 3-pounders, the ship's guns were loaded with roundshot instead of grape, or they could have been swept off the shore at one throw. The broadside must have been pretty poorly aimed, too, as it had little effect on the exposed 3 pounders (not much assurance if you were one of the affected), but during the distraction, Arnold quietly brought up his two 6-pounders where they could fire on the stern of the ship, raking her lengthwise with their greater power. In this case, 6-pounders firing lengthwise through the ship could cause significant mischief. Arnold also had Simcoe's Hessian riflemen work their way close through a series of ditches and they snuck to within 30 yards of the ship. There, they opened fire on the men on deck, and in minutes life on the Tempest was considerably hotter.

The other ships opened fire to support Tempest, and an unlucky shot broke one of Tempest's spring cables. Now drifting on a single anchor, Tempest was unable to train her guns on anyone. Under intense fire from Arnold's cannon and rifles, the sailors abandoned ship. The Hessians peppered them mercilessly in their boat until they surrendered and rowed ashore.

Recovering the ship's boat, Queen's Ranger Lt. Fitzpatrick, volunteer Armstrong, and 12 Rangers rowed toward the furthest ship after dropping off Capt. M'Kay and his Highlanders aboard Tempest. The Virginians began scuttling their ships and setting them afire. One blew up near the Tempest, setting some of the sails afire. The Highlanders cut the cable, fought the blaze and secured the Tempest as a prize.

Meanwhile, Fitzpatrick, under fire from shore, rowed and dropped men to fight the blazes on the other ships, cutting their cables in order to beach them. Armstrong and three men were dropped off on one ship, but its fire quickly got out of hand. Armstrong swam to shore and brought a boat back to pull his men off. As they were rowing away the ship exploded and sank.

Fitzpatrick brought in the ship he boarded. In all, the Rangers under Arnold participated in taking one 20-gun ship, a 16-gun brig, two lesser ships and a sloop, while ensuring the rest of the fleet was burnt or scuttled. The Virginians escaped their vessels and fled to the opposite shore, but none of the fleet escaped. The British captured 12 vessels in total, which the Virginians had been unable to destroy. ([1, 13]) Thus in one blow, almost the entire navy of the State of Virginia was destroyed. Left with one ship, they at last had one full compliment of men! The one ship left to Virginia—Liberty—was used as a transport for men and supplies in the work supplying the siege of Yorktown.

Liberty remained in Virginia service as a revenue cutter after the peace with permission of Congress, and saw the most service of any state or Continental vessel in the Revolution serving Virginia from 1775 to 1787.

The Small Unit Advantage

Thus the Queen's Rangers operated, either as a detached unit sent off on a specific mission or part of a larger army under higher command. In whatever task assigned, they did their part well.

Likely unappreciated at the time, the Queen's Rangers regularly employed to great advantage the most up-to-date advanced improvements in British arms in both the 3-pound Grasshopper and the Pattern 1776 rifles—one the first breechloading rifle ever employed in combat.

The little Grasshoppers proved ideal for a small corps like the Rangers and Simcoe used them with telling effect, even firing but one shot. Artillery allowed Simcoe to give the impression he was a more formidable force than his opponent suspected. A rapidly moving, fast-firing Grasshopper might just presage larger guns ponderously moving up behind, and caused opponents to seriously consider their situation—fight or flight?

Normally, a Royal Artillery crew was detached to work the gun, and normally there were at least two guns deployed as a battery. Each gun could be run with as few as two or three trained artillerymen, but they'd be slow to reload and repoint. Ideally, a crew of seven, eight or 12 under a non-commissioned officer were needed to load, aim and fire a gun at full speed, with a subaltern to supervise the two gun crews.

For the most part, Simcoe notes in his *Journal* only one gun being fired in his various actions. While 12 men may seem a huge resource for such a little piece, they were mostly employed in running the gun back up and aiming it. It wouldn't take many to prepare to fire the one shot Simcoe normally called for. As another option, a Commander could detail infantry to assist or even be the gunners, but this wasn't always a good option for the Rangers.

On one operation, Simcoe left the guns at the artillery park when it was suggested he use some of his men on the guns after instruction by the Royal Artillery. "[T]his Lt. Col. Simcoe declined. His corps was weak in numbers, and he considered the number of men, who must have attended his guns, more useful with their muskets: while the corps acted separately, cannon always furnished a reason for an enemy to avoid action. In some situations, even such contemptible guns as three-pounders might be of great use, in particular, in defence of a house or any position which might enable a corps, in case of necessity, to rally…" [1]

It worked both ways. Patrick Ferguson was dogging a Colonial column with 40 of his riflemen prior to the Battle of Brandywine and later wrote, "The army had by this time arrived at the place from whence we had discovered this Column and did us the honor of pointing two field pieces at which we begd leave to decline." Artillery had that effect. [2]

Guns were discharged with portfires held in a stave (middle). The linstock (nearest the wheel) holding slowmatch was kept in the rear to light the portfire. The portfire (a large spluttering punk) burned for about 15 or 20 minutes.

Rifles, Rangers & Revolution

Chapter 26
One Effective Insect
The Grasshopper re-imagined.

WHICH BRINGS US to our little gun built around the turn of the 21st century. The barrel most closely resembles the design of Col. James Pattison among the first guns cast by the Verbruggens. Cast of iron by South Bend Replicas, the barrel is 37 inches long and has most features of the Pattison. The cascabel (the round knob at the back of the barrel) is missing the Pattison's characteristic flat spot that rests on the elevation screw, (although its lack matches published ordnance drawings). (4, 11) The barrel is steel lined, and has a 2¼-inch bore rather than the 2.77-inch of the 3-pounder. In reality, it is a 1-pounder, but far easier to feed, since 2-inch steel shot is available. I haven't weighed this particular barrel, but the weight of the original Pattison barrel is about 210 pounds.

The barrel rests in deep U-cuts in the trail arms and held in place by hinged iron straps fitting over iron loops through which "L" shaped self-tightening keys are driven. The barrel can be easily and quickly hoisted off. Congreve barrels were in the same weight range with a length of 40½ inches. Weight of the entire gun is roughly 800 pounds. Originally, bronze cost about six times that of iron, and that ratio is pretty much still true today. Only kings and rich men have guns cast of bronze! The Royal Navy used iron guns for the same reason.

The carriage was made to British plans by the late owners of Cannons Ltd., in the pattern of the Grasshopper, whose signature is the brackets on the front and back of the carriage allowing it to be lifted and moved about in the "Irish Carry" method using four staves. Two staves were bent, and two were straight. Inserted into the brackets, the angle of the bent ones makes the gun look like it has "grasshopper" legs, but they allow the gun to carried more comfortably with even weight distribution by keeping the staves level over the shoulders of the men. "Comfortable" is relative, of course, and it is doubtful the whole gun was carried far this way—if it ever was—off the parade ground. You have to use 8 men of equal height, too.

There are two brackets at each stave point (a total of eight) and the four rearmost brackets are pierced for a pin held to the gun by a chain. When the staves are inserted for "Irish Carry," the pins trap them so a stave can't be inadvertently pulled free dropping the gun unceremoniously.

The carriage itself is designed to be easily broken down into its component parts. The wheels have quick knock offs so they can be removed quickly, in addition to two hooked rope points on both hubs for hauling and aiming. Two big bolts hold the axle crossmember to the trail. The bolts are locked by early-style square, "lock washers" having a taper in width so tightening the nut twists the bolt slightly to prevent loosening. The Grasshopper gun can be broken down to six components for ease of movement: Barrel, trail, axel, two wheels and ammo box, all of which are light enough to be carried on narrow paths.

Various ringbolts along the side are for tying the loading and cleaning implements with leather belts. The ammunition chest rides behind the barrel between the trails, and it only fits one way since its body is slightly wider at the back than at the front matching the arms of the trail. The ammo chest lifts off the trail to be carried behind the gun using big, brass handles. It is built to modern cannon rules with a lid incapable of opening beyond 45 degrees or remaining open.

I haven't even scratched the surface of implements kept on hand to run this gun. As a pleasure exercise, firing the gun can be done with little preparation and by two people. Firing the gun the way it was used in battle requires a lot more preparation, a bigger crew (24 men for a battery of two, guns including a subaltern), and far more preparation if horses are involved (as many as three depending on ammunition load). That many men allowed for attrition and rapid firing, but the gun could still be served by as few as two.

THE PATTISON GRASSHOPPER was a short-range gun. Maximum range was a 1,000 yards with roundshot, and canister much closer beginning around 350 yards. The chances of becoming overrun were now very high, and gunners had to be prepared to spike the guns and scoot. A hammer drove an iron nail (with a fish hook at the tip) into the touch hole to render the gun unusable so they weren't turned on the retreating army. Guns were often captured and recaptured during the war, sometimes in the same battle.

Aiming the little guns wasn't very sophisticated. After leveling, the gunner pointed the piece by eye alone. The little guns had no sights, the range was estimated and the elevation chosen from a table. Placing the "Gunner's Quadrant" in the muzzle, the degree of elevation the table indicated was set using the plumb bob.

Elevation was adjusted by turning the brass wheel. Windage was adjusted by inserting a long wooden stave locked with the pin for the gunner to point the Grasshopper. The hole in the trail crossmember attaches the gun to the limber, and the iron brackets allow the gun to be carried by men or attached to one horse and then called a "Galloper." The gun was not raised above 3° elevation as a rule. The point was to skip the little iron ball through a formation and the range with one or two skips could be 800 to 1,000 yards. Case or canister loaded with musket balls was best at 150 yards (not much time to scoot!) and modestly effective out to 350 yards.

Rifles, Rangers & Revolution

Chapter 27
The Price of Poundage
Moving iron is hard work!

GEN. PATTISON, DESIGNER of the Grasshopper carriage, tried to think of every logistical problem faced by troops with artillery along on a mission. As usual, for all the good ideas in the design, when commanders on the ground were faced with moving artillery over uncertain terrain, their attitudes were indifferent to the possibilities built into the gun faced with the level of work involved. In a letter to Lieutenant-Colonel Bolton, commanding at Niagara dated August 26th, 1779, from Colonel John Butler of the notorious Butler's Rangers (whose reputation became the antithesis of the Queen's Rangers), Butler said, "As to the two Grasshoppers, besides the great difficulty there would be to carry them along with suitable Ammunition, I believe they would be of no very material Service in the Woods…" [4]

I've yet to find an account of the Grasshoppers being manhandled through difficult terrain via "Irish Carry." Its hard to believe any place that a pack horse couldn't go, eight men could. It would be easier to carry the gun in pieces over a difficult obstacle and a narrow path would require such an action. Simcoe notes the gun was "carried down" to the banks of the river, but they likely used ropes to ease it down rather than disassembly.

That carrying it disassembled could be done is shown in drawings in *Grasshoppers and Butterflies*.[11] The Queen's Rangers are pictured transporting the Butterfly completely disassembled using 16 men. This would seem a sure way to get the gun over treacherous ground pack horses couldn't go (especially if you didn't have many horses). The Royal Artillery method shows the carriage left assembled, so less time would be needed to get the gun back into action.

Of course, on trails only as wide as a single file, the gun would have to be knocked down entirely to move it. But you had to really want artillery to justify such effort. Even if you could move the gun up along narrow trails, you would have to leave your baggage wagons behind. If the attack failed, there probably wouldn't be time to knock the gun apart to bring it back to the wagons, either. Where this carry system would prove handy is moving an artillery battery to a far flung forward outpost or fort with poor or no roads.

On the Patriot side, Francis Marion, "The Swamp Fox" himself, had two Grasshoppers with him in South Carolina when he heard Major Wemyss, late commander of the Queen's Rangers, now of the 63rd and a large body of

Firing the little Grasshopper required (clockwise from left) a leather cartouche to carry the charge from magazine to muzzle (the red "8" indicates a full charge), cannon balls strapped to sabots, case shot nailed to sabots, a pick to pierce the cartridge bag, tin fuse, and hammer and spikes to "spike the gun" in the event of being overrun. Behind these are a portfire and stave atop the linstock. Guns were fired only by the portfire, and the linstock only used to light the portfire.

Tories were on his trail. Down to 150 men, Marion sent Major James to scout the British. Upon hearing he was greatly outnumbered, Marion ordered a retreat. "About half of his party left him. They could not leave their properties and their families at the discretion of an irritated, relentless enemy... Marion's march was for some time much impeded by the two field-pieces which he attempted to take along, so after crossing the Little Pee Dee he wheeled them off to the side of the road and left them in a swamp. He never afterwards encumbered himself with artillery." [5]

The little guns could carry a maximum of 60 rounds of ammunition depending on its configuration. Ammunition for the 3-pounders came fixed. "Fixed" ammunition entailed solid iron shot strapped to wooden sabots with tin. Case shot was a tin can loaded with musket balls. No exploding shells or grapeshot were made for these guns.

To make cartridges, flannel was rolled around formers then sewn together. The powder was pre-weighed and put into the cartridges. Ignition was by pre-made goose quill or tin fuses with powder glued in. Quill fuses were consumed by ignition, but tin fuses would be ejected upon firing. They could be reused if recovered and not too damaged. The base of the flannel cartridges tended to blow off and stick in the bore. These had to be fished out periodically using the patch worm.

The Grasshopper's single trail-mounted ammunition box would be removed well behind the gun in the field. If the gun was a Butterfly, the axle-mounted side boxes holding 20 rounds each would be removed to the rear. One box held the cartridges and the other the shot. Upon firing, the gun recoiled four to six feet. Sponging between shots, a good, full crew of seven or eight men (and up to 12) could fire as many as eight to 10 shots a minute. The extra men helped re-point the gun faster. The gun could be served by as few as two men.

And a gun could be loaded simply, too. A ladle was carried so loose powder could be put into the bore. The ladle was filled with the correct amount of powder, run all the way down the barrel and rotated 180 degrees.

Highly dangerous, this method called for an open keg of powder nearby with burning linstocks and port fires around, not to mention your opponent's cannon balls whizzing past. Instead of cannon balls strapped to sabots, a wad of waste could be rammed down over the charge, the ball rolled in and more waste placed on top to hold the ball in place. Pour powder from the Gunner's horn into the touchhole and apply the fire. Run out of case? Pebbles, rocks, nails and other scrap metal could be used in a pinch. Lacking case shot in a defensive position, Simcoe once arranged piles of rocks and aimed guns loaded with roundshot at them. A hit would explode the piles like shrapnel.

After the war, many captured guns served with the American army, and were distributed among the principal arsenals or sent to the frontier. Some in British hands served on the new frontier at Niagara and Detroit. Many would fight Napoleon in Spain, and some would return for the War of 1812. None are reported in England today.

In an odd note, many guns of all calibers captured by the Americans were engraved with the victorious action at which they were supposedly captured. Not surprisingly, such guns are in greater number than guns actually captured. When activity on the frontier demanded, and especially when the War of 1812 broke out, America was (as usual in those days) in need of guns badly, and many of these engraved guns saw action once again.

Examples of all three 3-pounder types still exist in museums in the U.S. and Canada. Surprisingly, they all managed to survive being scrapped for their metal to supply the various conflicts the United States and Canada were involved in over the years. The ones in the U.S. were headed for the smelters at the start of WW II, and it took an Act of Congress to save them.

Chapter 28
Manning a Gun
A glimpse at the tools of the trade.

SAFETY WAS A serious consideration among gunners and all the more extraordinary when you remember the wounded were left behind on the battlefield as so much rubbish. Artillerymen were well drilled though and not easily replaced. The Artillery Park opened a laboratory when it was set up, since the various mixtures necessary for making slow match, portfires, carcasses (incendiary shells) and other specialty fireworks were made on site. Only powder and shot were shipped. The artillerymen rarely had idle hands.

Up to the time of the American Revolution, powder was ladled from open kegs into the bore. This is highly dangerous, since an open keg is around spluttering fireworks. Paper cartridges were used at first but left behind burning bits hard to extinguish. Cloth bags became standard for the army around the time of the Revolution and remained so until the arrival of metallic cartridges.

The cartridge bags were hand sewn by artillerymen. Favored material for bags was wool serge, but could be whatever was available. The material was sewn around a former of bore size with a circular piece of material sewn for the bottom. After filling with powder, the ends were sewn over. For the 3 pounder, a ½ or ¾ charge was provided to help adjust range. Rather than sew different length bags, wad material (usually scraps of cloth or tow) was stuffed in the take up the space. The amount of powder was then painted on the bottom by weight ("8," "6," "5," or "4" denoted how many ounces of powder was in the bag and also helped the gunner know which end to put into the muzzle so the end with the powder ended up at the breech.

The sewn end had a habit of blowing off and getting left behind smoldering away, which is why the bore was sponged thoroughly every time and wormed every three shots. All this was done in the pressure of battle, too. Nothing like taking your time in a hurry!

Historian Rick Hatton, a member of the Royal Artillery Museum, was kind enough to share his research, which filled in gaps left by other existing records. The *U.S. Army's 1850 Ordnance Manual* has very detailed instructions, too, and I suspect not much had changed in the intervening years. This would be one of the doldrums of artillery life, but considering how few entertainments were available, it would certainly pass the time!

Gunners first chipped the rust from the roundshot, then gauged them to ensure they would fit the bore, then painted them black to prevent more rust forming. The shot was strapped with tin secured by nails to a wooden sabot.

For the 3-pounder Grasshopper, the propellant part was stored separately. Some bigger guns had the powder bags fixed to the sabot with the round shot or the tin case shot on top for faster, if more dangerous loading.

Fuses were made from goose quills or tin tubes filled with powder. On either, a drop of glue sealed both ends against moisture and prevented the powder dribbling out. The tin tubes had a funnel shape soldered to the end. This blew the tube free on discharge. If recovered sufficiently undamaged, it could be reused.

Preparing for battle, the ammunition chest was moved 25 feet to the back of the gun. The powder man went to the chest and was handed a cartridge which he put into a "cartouche" which was a leather bucket with lid. He would run the load the gunner called for to the muzzle for the loader. This protected the explosive from stray sparks from the linstock or portfire. The layers of safety developed for loading and firing these guns was extensively thought out.

British artillerymen were highly trained and disciplined. War was already a dangerous business, and they learned early on not to defeat themselves with accidents. From the get-go, American artillery took many of these lessons to heart, and earned the respect of their opponents.

After the battle at Fort Klock, Oct. 19, 1780, British General Sir John Johnson abandoned his 3-pound gun and baggage. The Americans took an inventory of the everything with the gun, giving us a glimpse into what the crew kept on hand. [6]:

A Return of Ordinance & Stores taken from the British army, Comm'd by Sir John Johnston, [sic] *Fort Rensselaer Oct'r 19th, 1780*
1 Piece Brass Ordinanc 3 pd. with Emplim'ts Comp.; 23 Rounds, Round Shott fix's; 10 ditto Canister; 1 Quadrant; 2 Powder measures; 1 hand saw; 1 four pd. wt.; 1 half ditto; 1 Quarttr ditto, 1 Scale beam; 1 mallet & set; 20 fuses; 1 Seane marlin; 2 Port fires; 1 Cole Chisel; 1 auger; 1 Punch; 1 Seane Quick match; 100 wt. Corn Powder; Drudging box.
Jo. Driskill Lieut Artillery

Translator's Note

Near the bottom are some confusing terms: "1 Seane marlin; 1 Seane Quick match; and a Drudging box." This list is from The Public Papers of George Clinton, First Governor of New York, published in 1900. But what's a Seane? The mistake in these phrases possibly occurred while trying to decipher the original handwritten copy on top of being creatively spelled or illegible.

Driskill likely meant "Skein" although several other definitions popped up during the Easter egg hunt through several dictionaries. *Webster's Dictionary of the English language 1828* [7] spells it "skain" and if Lt. Driskill's first "e" is really a poorly written "c" you can easily see "Skein" creatively spelled as "Scane" if Driskill spelled it phonetically, and later interpreted as "Seane." A skein is roughly 120 yards of material, and would be about right for an amount of slow match and "marlin."

"Marlin" is "marline" misspelled. *Webster's 1828* defines marline as, "A small line composed of two strands little twisted, and either tarred or white; used for winding round ropes and cables, to prevent their being fretted by the blocks, etc." Plenty of rope was standard issue with guns, and a skein of marline would prove very useful. "Drudge box" is Dredge-box misspelled. A dredge-box was used in the making of quick match.

In examining the list above, it is apparent the gun was in action, and fired more case shot than roundshot. A list titled *"A Proportion of Stores for Twenty-four Light Three Pounders mounted on Colonel Pattison's Carriage [with] Three Pounder Light Brass Guns With Traveling Carriages and Limbers"* in *Grasshoppers and Butterflies* [11] shows each gun would ideally have ready to be drawn upon: 200 roundshot fixed to wood bottoms; 200 flannel cartridges filled; 400 Tin Case, fixed as above; 660 tin tubes [fuses]; 2 Tube boxes with straps; 50 portfires, and 2 portfire staves. The maximum ammunition load was usually no more than 60 rounds, and likely less depending on the mission and how quickly the battery had to move.

The list shows enough material to outfit each gun for three or four missions. The big takeaway is how much Case Shot was issued compared to roundshot. Twice as much anti-personnel case shot went with the guns, and Lt. Driskoll notes: *23 Rounds, Round Shott fix's; 10 ditto Canister,* indicating the gun had fired more canister (or case shot) than roundshot.

The gun was down to two portfires, so they had been ready for action or in action for some time.

The King's Colours of the Queen's Rangers are hand painted on silk. The unit's original name included the "1st American Regiment" and it is a name the regiment uses to this day. (There were five loyalist regiments raised in the war.) These are believed to be the oldest military colours in North America, and were carried by the Rangers in open battle. The colours are not on public display, and their presentation here is courtesy of the Queen's York Rangers. Photo by Anne de Haas for Art In Arms Press, courtesy of the Queen's York Rangers.

Chapter 29
Yorktown
The beginning of the end of British rule.

THE COLOURS OF the Queen's Rangers were furled for the last time on October 19, 1781 when Lord Cornwallis surrendered at Yorktown, Virginia. Cornwallis sent Simcoe (whose health had deteriorated in the months since Spencer's Ordinary) and many loyalist Rangers, including the riflemen and others who possibly faced execution by the Americans on the one ship he was granted. All were allowed to sail under arms to Canada, and Simcoe took his colors. The Queen's Rangers had never lost a battle when acting alone, and it must have rankled to surrender.

Perhaps the greatest praise Simcoe received came from the esteemed American cavalry officer "Lighthorse" Harry Lee, who commanded Lee's Legion of cavalry and infantry, one of the finest Continental light companies—and whom Simcoe had successfully impersonated twice. Lee's Legion performed duty similar to the Rangers for America, and in his memoir, Lee said about Simcoe, "This officer commanded a legionary corps called the Queen's Rangers, and had during the war signalised himself on various occasions. He was a man of letters, and like the Romans and Grecians, cultivated science amid the turmoil of camp. He was enterprising, resolute, and persevering; weighing well his project before entered upon, and promptly seizing every advantage which offered in the course of execution." [1]

As a partisan corps, the officers of the Queen's Rangers, who volunteered from other regiments, were promoted one rank from the one they left, and reverted to their original rank on release. The rank and file were simply released. Upon Simcoe's representation to the King, the ranks of the Ranger officers were made permanent, and all other ranks were honorably enrolled in the British Army. The Rangers were officially disbanded by Britain in 1783 [9], and the men and officers settled on lands in Nova Scotia (although you'd think a unit serving as well as the Rangers would be worth keeping intact).

The Rangers were reformed by Simcoe after his appointment as Lt. Governor of Upper Canada in 1790. Only a few of the P1776 rifles brought into Canada with the repatriated Rangers still exist. The rifles had been converted to percussion with their rammer/swivel mechanism removed, possibly proving its fragility, or simply a lack of spare parts. Not a bad legacy

John Graves Simcoe became the first Governor of Upper Canada, and upon his retirement the colours were hung in the Great Hall of his estate at Wolford near Honiton in Devonshire, England. They remained in possession of the Simcoe family until being brought to Canada in the 1920s. In the mid 1970s, both colours were restored for the 200th Anniversary of the formation of the Queen's Rangers. The colors had suffered over the more than 200 years since they had been last furled, and were painstakingly stabilized and mounted by the Royal Ontario Museum. They are currently on display in the Officer's Mess of the Queen's York Rangers based in Toronto, Canada. Photo by Anne de Haas for Art In Arms Press.

for the King's first rifle, or any rifle for that matter! Only one of the Birmingham-made flintlocks is known in its original condition, and at least one of the Huhnstock rifles survives.

The Rangers again reformed for the Canadian Rebellion of 1837 as militia raised and commanded by Samuel Jarvis, who was the son of William Jarvis, an original officer in the Queen's Rangers. They reformed to serve in WW I and WW II. Recently, the Queen's York Rangers, 1st American Regiment, have served on operations in Afghanistan, Kosovo, Bosnia, Croatia, Somalia, Namibia and Cyprus.

Return of the Colors

The original colors of the Queen's Rangers were brought to Canada from England in the early 1920's. They were stabilized, restored, and framed by the Royal Ontario Museum in the 1970s and are on display at the Officer's Mess of the Queen's York Rangers at the Fort York Armoury, Toronto, Ontario. They are believed to be the oldest military colors in North America.

They hadn't been photographed or otherwise recorded until Art in Arms Press commissioned photographer Anne de Haas in September 2018 to photograph them in situ with the courtesy and cooperation of the Queen's York Rangers. Since their restoration, they have never been on public display until posted to the Art In Arms Press website on September 28, 2018—237 years after they were last unfurled at Yorktown.

Sadly, the little cannon so capably used, the rifle deployed so artfully, and the unit commanded so well, were all consigned to the dustbin after the war. The Ferguson rifle never was able to fully display its versatile prowess, or it might have revolutionized war. The carefully thought out "one size fits all" rifle was supplanted by purpose built ones for infantry and cavalry once use of the rifle was better appreciated during the next conflict.

The 3-pounder gun easier to transport to far-flung battlefields with a barrel weight of 210 pounds-plus vs. 1,200 pounds-plus for a 12-pounder, lacked the power to accomplish much of what artillery is called on to do, especially facing the bigger guns.

The British used 3-pounders during the Napoleonic Wars, mostly in Spain during Wellington's Peninsular campaign, but they were easily outranged. They arrived in America again for the War of 1812. Even the 6-pounder proved too small (except in America), and the 12-pounder would become the standard from the Napoleonic War until after the American Civil War when the shell-firing breechloader supplanted muzzleloaders forever.

It is oft said the lessons learned about the value of rifles in the American Revolution were thrown away by the British Army, but they were just mislaid for awhile (something habitual with the British). The seeds were sown, and soon began to germinate. The literacy rate of the officer class was high, and many of these men wrote about their experiences.

Hessian Jäger Captain Johann von Ewald, who often served with the Queen's Rangers wrote the *Treatise on Partisan Warfare* in 1785, and it was eagerly read by none other than the Duke of York—Frederick Augustus of the House of Hanover (the German province where many Hessian Jäger regiments were raised). The Duke was King George III's 2nd son, and began the task of reorganization of the British army after suffering several embarrassing losses to France's Revolutionary Army (or rather, mob) in the 1790s.

While the loss of America was a stunning blow to the Crown (and especially the treasury), the works of Ewald were the beginning of new thinking in Light Infantry tactics and armaments. Another enthusiastic student of Light Infantry was General Sir John Moore, who took the writings of Ewald's and others to heart culminating in the formation of the Experimental Corps of Rifles, later gaining fame as the 95th Rifles and issued the newly-designed Baker Pattern 1800 rifle (this time the rifle got a patchbox), as well as Baker-armed companies of light infantry in several other regiments. The Baker rifle's construction and mission was thoroughly thought out reflecting the lessons learned.

Under the Duke of York, the British Army was reorganized into a new professional force, one willing to recognize merit with promotion into the officer class from the ranks instead only by patronage as before. The studious use of the rifle in the hands of the individual soldiers began the realization that even the common soldiers were of more value than previously thought.

The revitalized army developed new tactics and technology just in time to face off against a new menace. Far more insidious and dangerous than the American colonists, the little captain of artillery—Napoleon Bonaparte—conquered much of Europe, and may have conquered the world had not Britain stood firmly in his way. Such prowess didn't come easily, but its foundation had been laid during the American Revolution.

Rifles, Rangers & Revolution

Part IV: Repros at the Range
Chapter 30
The Ferguson
Easy to shoot, accurate to boot!

WHAT A PLEASANT rifle to load and shoot! Accurate, too. The manual of arms is simpler than that of a musket and much simpler than a muzzleloading rifle's. Unscrew the breech, drop a lubricated ball into the chamber, push it forward with your pinky, close the breech, prime and fire. Sometimes a little too much powder is poured in the back. No matter, it rises with the breech screw and can be swept into the pan as priming. One less motion.

Looking at the Ferguson on paper, one would assume the ball would be of groove size, or about .65 caliber. Back in the day, this would have meant providing a ball unique to the Ferguson. Those who have shot the rifle this way say gas blowback through the breech screw is unpleasantly severe, and accuracy so-so. Historian Ricky Roberts notes in his book *Every Insult and Indignity* that it was highly unlikely Ferguson would build his breechloader around special ammunition. The British carbine ball, nominally .615 inch and weighing 344 grains, was the logical choice and the one around which the P1776 muzzleloader was rifled.

Ricky found using those balls lubed with tallow/beeswax—which would be other common ingredients available—extends the number of accurate shots that can be taken far beyond any other rifle fired with period lubricants, and reduces the amount of gas leakage suffered. These carbine balls are only .005 inch larger than the .610-inch bore size of the Ferguson. Ricky uses a more economical easier to obtain lube of 2:1 beeswax/vegetable shortening. I've been using beeswax/tallow more out of tradition, but if tallow becomes hard to find, I won't hesitate to try shortening.

But there are no properly sized "carbine balls" available commercially. Jeff Tanner Moulds in England offers single cavity brass molds at reasonable prices and with a quick turnaround. His molds fit common handles (like Lee) and all you need to add is pair of cutters for the sprue. A double boiler is the best choice to melt the beeswax/tallow mixture, and I dipped them with a pair of needlenose pliers after cutting the sprue. Doing so, you can shoot all day. Whether it was possible for the men to dip balls in lube is not recorded. Possibly they rolled balls in softened lube of some sort in the tin tray of their cartridge boxes, maybe only with beeswax in a pinch, but some sort of lube is

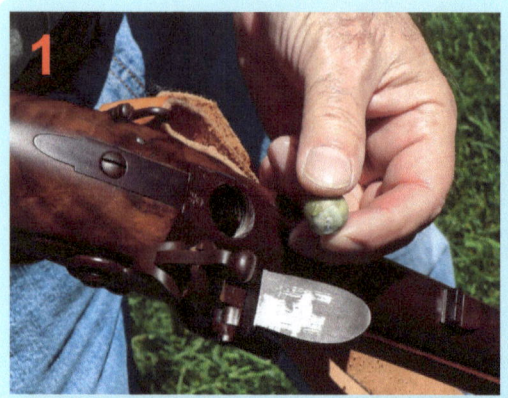
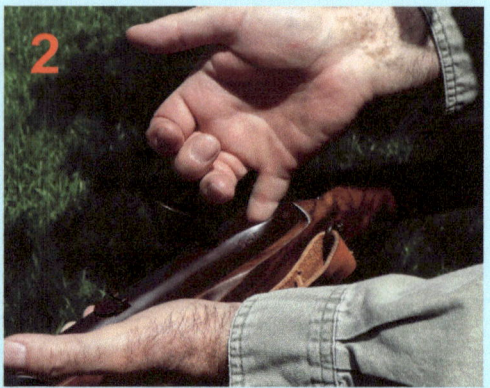

LOADING THE FERGUSON is simple and fast. Drop in a ball (1), push it in with your pinky (2), Pour in powder (3). Ferguson's riflemen would load from the horn, but you'll need to load from a measure or charger at most ranges. Turn the screw up and sweep off excess into the pan to prime (4). Note in this case far too much powder is pooled around the breech screw. It's not hard to do, but the excess powder quickly fouls the breech causing hard operation. Loading quickly, with the large excess swept off into the pan, the gun became frozen during the chronograph test in just five shots. Still, that's five fast, accurate shots, and something unheard of in the day. A better way is to use a charger and drop in just enough powder so little excess comes out the top, then prime separately. Doing so, I only have to clean the breech screw every seven or 12 shots, but of course that slows down the rate of fire—the big reason to use this rifle. This particular problem would be exacerbated by combat, and very likely one of the main reasons the technology wasn't fully explored. No hat (5). A hat brim funnels hot gas escaping from the breech screw into your face. It's another one of those annoyances that would have been addressed if the rifle was adopted into service. Photos: Roger Renner

Rifles, Rangers & Revolution

This is a 3¼-inch group fired at 100-yards from a rest. The .615-inch ball was greased with tallow/beeswax over 50 grains of FFFg powder.

necessary.

Loading is fast and effortless. The coarse threads on the breech screw require only one full turn to open—one reason why the gun is fast—but it is important the rifleman not rotate the lever too far on opening or the breech screw will drop free. This can happen by tilting the rifle a trifle with the lever all the way open, as I found out. It would not surprise me if a few Fergusons became so disabled in the heat of a fight.

A curious modern problem is when your public range doesn't allow you the full range of motion for effortless loading. My local range prohibits pointing the muzzle down far enough to fill the chamber and close the breech screw because the concrete pads extend beyond the benches, end in a curb, and a ricochet could be dangerous. On such a shallow angle it is easy to overcharge with powder. While it makes priming effortless, spilt powder gets into the threads of the breech screw necessitating more frequent cleaning there.

A tedious workaround for me was to raise the breech screw halfway, trap it with my left hand, and tilt the gun up while putting the powder charger into the smaller opening. I never had to swab the bore during any of my range sessions, but I did have to clean the breech screw more often when I overcharged the chamber. At the first session, all shots fell accurately on the target 50 yards away. The first three cut the "X" of a blue Birchwood-Casey target. Recoil was negligible, and gas blowby annoying.

At 100 yards, I put three shots into 3¼ inches. There are many moving parts while shooting flintlocks, and accuracy is dependent on all those coming together. What makes the Ferguson special is my ability to hold deteriorates faster than the rifle's ability to deliver the ball accurately.

After coming home with the thoroughly dirtied Ferguson, I carefully worked the action from the stock. Care is needed, since the Ferguson's weak spot is the lock area of the stock. Havoc ensues if the barrel is used as leverage. The wood-to-metal fit is crucial to longevity. This rifle will endure, because the

Rifle Shoppe glass-bedded it from breech to muzzle, and it is very tight in the stock. A purist may wince, but at what these cost, the use of glass is welcome, since the gun has to come out of the wood to be cleaned properly. At the Shoppe's suggestion, I had a wooden dowel turned to fit the screw breech section to help coax out the action straight down out of the stock.

And does the barrel ever foul! With the breech in a bucket of water, I couldn't get the first patch down the barrel. Black powder fouling turns into cement in the low humidity here, although the accuracy was surprisingly and happily unaffected the entire time. Pouring a cup of extra hot water down the barrel first helps, as does Dawn dish soap. Beware of scalding water and hot metal. The barrel gets hot enough from tap water to get uncomfortable, but the hottest water you can use is the key to quickly clean a Ferguson.

Powder Charges & Chamber Pressures

Ferguson also had the brilliant idea to reduce the powder charge. This was economical, reduced chamber pressure further in conjunction with the bore-size ball, and helped mitigate the amount of gas blowing back out of the action. In those days, a powder charge was calculated as a fraction of the weight of the ball. A $1/5$ charge was considered a standard target load, and this is the charge Ferguson chose. A standard "service charge" would normally be $1/4$ or $1/3$ of the 344-grain ball. Jess Melot measured the original's chamber and gave his Ferguson a similar 65 grains of powder. That works out to about a $1/5$ charge. The arm also has a tapered chamber, which helps center the ball. Either my pinky is too short to push the ball all the way in or the thickness of the dip-lubed balls won't allow them to go farther, so my charge is usually about 50 grains. The savings in powder consumed is an overlooked advantage to the Ferguson, but one that would have provided real savings in scale.

While rifle powder was much more expensive compared to musket powder, the standard musket cartridge held 170 grains of powder—almost thrice the Ferguson charge. The Ferguson didn't need paper cartridges rolled, either, just lubricated balls. The carbine ball was another savings in that it weighed about $1/3$ less than the musket ball. This isn't a trivial savings when the scale of armies living on supplies brought by ship, and moved by horse and oxen-drawn wagons. It would increase the ammunition load of the soldier, and his ammo wouldn't decay from a march (but the lube might melt and glue it all together).

Shooting the Ferguson is far faster than shooting a conventional rifle and faster than shooting a musket or even a percussion rifle. As nascent technology, it was never developed beyond the 100 rifles issued during the Revolutionary War, or warfare might have gotten very ugly a lot sooner!

CLEANING THE FERGUSON RIFLE presents special maintenance problems almost insurmountable in its day. It wouldn't be surprising to learn this was another major consideration leading to its abandonment, since doctrine was to leave the rifle assembled. Fieldstripping requires great care and patience, but the cleaning is then straightforward. First, half cock the hammer and remove the single lock screw from the face of the lock plate. Gently remove the lock, taking care not to damage the inletting. (1) Remove the breech screw, remove the top tang screw. Note the fragility of the wood in this area. Next, drive out the three slides holding the barrel to the stock. Now you must take GREAT CARE! Turn over the rifle and carefully work the barreled action from the stock taking great pains NOT to use the barrel for leverage. Doing so will destroy the stock mortise in which the breech resides. A piece of 1-inch dowel turned down to fit the breech helps (2). Note the action is fully glass bedded. (3). The rifle disassembled (4). The sling can be left in place during disassembly (a nice touch on both 1776 rifles). Reassembly: With the barrel on your table, carefully place and push the wood straight down onto the breech. The wood is easier to keep from canting than the barrel assembly. Push straight down. Stop if it feels wrong. Note: The breech screw only goes in one way, so watch where it exits. Hint: It's just off center to the left. Yes, it can drive you crazy.

Chapter 31
Shooting The Pattern 1776
A (not so) "common" muzzleloading rifle.

ONLY A FEW Pattern 1776 rifles are left and most of those were converted to percussion in their working life. Owning, let alone shooting an original is off the table, but the kit by The Rifle Shoppe made the molds and stock pattern from the most complete original flintlock known. One downside is that the P1776 kit comes with a .62-caliber Colerain barrel with round-bottom grooves rather than the original's square-bottom ones. The muzzle of this rifle isn't "coned" to replicate the way an original accepted a press-fit patched ball, (and after shooting it, it shoots so well I won't chance coning). Colerain implores people to shoot the rifle before coning in order to have a baseline for accuracy, as coning can destroy accuracy if done improperly. So no attempt on my part can replicate actual performance, but the gun handles and feels the way an original would, so we'll discuss those areas.

With a broad, well-shaped musket-style buttplate, the P1776 is very pleasant to shoot, even with a hefty charge of 85 grains of FFFg (a ¼ charge by weight of ball) under a .600-inch 325-grain roundball and a .010-inch patch. The .600 was easier to load than a .610, and shot just as well. Lehigh Valley Patch Lube was the go-to patch lube and the amazing stuff enabled me to shoot

The broad musket-style buttplate is comfortable even shooting 85-grain charges of FFFg. The fore-end palm swell is quite useful in giving the rifle the tight hold aiding accuracy.

without cleaning all day. Shooting 20 or 30 rounds per session, I never had a problem loading, even after prolonged ceasefires in the hot, dry air here in northern Nevada.

In those good ol' days, spit would have been used often, but the British would have had the ability to lube their patches with whale oil or tallow. Back East, where the humidity can keep fouling soft, you can get four or five shots off before you have to wipe the bore, but here in the arid West, you'll get maybe two before loading gets tough. The only thing equal to—or maybe even better—than Lehigh Valley Patch Lube is Sperm whale oil, but at the price it fetches these days, I'll stick with Lehigh. Anyone using whale oil on his patches would have had a smooth-running rifle, and whale oil—used in lamps—was readily available. Another benefit of whale oil is it excellent for lubrication and rust prevention.

I did try a ⅓ charge of about 70 grains with no success. This rifle likes the hefty service charge, and it is one that would serve well as a hunting load. The even, neutral balance of the rifle along with its short, handy length and 3-leaf sight would make a perfect hunting rifle. That makes sense, since the original was designed by a German gunsmith specializing in Jäger rifles. Under 85 grains of Goex FFFg, the ball handily breaks 1,400 feet per second and will approach 1,500 with Swiss. That should easily drop game out to 100 yards or more, and it is accurate enough to do so.

The target on the left was fired at 50 yards, and the one on the right at 100. The white Birchwood Casey Shoot-N-C targets give good contrast when using a center hold with the front sight rather than the usual 6 o'clock hold.

CLEANING IS SIMPLE. The muzzleloading P1776 was built along the lines of a fine sporting rifle rather than a military rifle. The barrel is held to the stock by three slides or keys that are pinned and won't become lost on removal. The barrel has a break-off breech, meaning once the slides are out, the barrel can be lifted out of the stock for cleaning. Note: The sling swivel does not have to be removed to remove the barrel.

First, remove the lock screws on the left side. Place one back in and gently tap on it to release the lock from its mortise. Carelessness here can damage the inletting, so be careful. Pull the rammer, and unscrew its brass retaining cap. Use a punch to drive the slides from their slots. Lift the barrel free from the stock at the muzzle. The breech of the barrel can be immersed in a bucket of very hot water (I add Dawn detergent) and cleaned by running a patch back and forth. The hydraulic pressure ensures a deep clean. Or use a quality commercial muzzleloading solvent like Birchwood Casey No. 77 Muzzle Magic or a similar one. Dry, oil and reassemble. The rammer may be used, and gives you appreciation of the original hardships, but a commercial rod and sized jag is preferable.

Rifles, Rangers & Revolution

Chapter 32
The Brown Bess
Repro quality levels.

THREE TIERS OF shootable reproduction Brown Bess muskets are on the market currently. The lowest price ones made in India start at around $500-600. Surprisingly, they are technically accurate, but the workmanship is execrable. They should be home-proved before shooting live ammunition.

At the high end of the reproductions are the USA-made Rifle Shoppe kits. (It is highly probable Rifle Shoppe guns were sent to India and replicated.) Rifle Shoppe kits are accurate and made from top-flight materials. Kits only, they require advanced building skills. If you hire someone to build one, expect the price to double, which is as expensive as a low-end original.

The Pedersoli reproduction is the most accessible, made of high-quality steel with a carefully bored barrel and will give years of service as well as look good on display. Pedersoli muskets routinely win the European smoothbore black powder championships, and why I chose not to tackle an Indian-made replica. However, their Brown Bess is not exactly representative of a particular period. It is seemingly meant to be a "bridge" gun for use by reenactors depicting either the F&I war or American Revolution, and is a hodgepodge design. The lock style is closer to the Rev War, but marked "Grice 1762" instead of "Tower." The "Crown over GR" and border engraving are cast in as well and all are rather crude looking. The top tang of the buttplate, designed to be simple to machine inlet, is unlike any ever fitted to a British arm, and nothing can be done for it unless wood is added to the top of the stock, something never entirely successful even with heroic effort. Other than the buttplate, the rest of the gun is a pretty good model of the Bess used in the Revolution. Barrels are straight and true and kept to consistent tolerances. Locks have hardened parts and overall construction shows care in the workmanship.

You're on your own buying an original. Many are put together from parts of many generations of Brown Bess muskets, sometimes in the period, but often in the present (or near present) as collectors assemble a complete gun from a pile of parts. A lot can happen to a gun over the 300 years since the first Bess saw service! Buy the book by Goldstein and Mowbray on the Bess, and consult reputable antique dealers if originals are in your sights. A good one will

The Pedersoli will deliver a decent group of 5 inches at 50 yards using a patched roundball. Such accuracy is adequate for hunting, and it wasn't unusual for frontiersmen to use a smoothbore. They were cheaper than rifles, and more versatile, since they doubled as a shotgun.

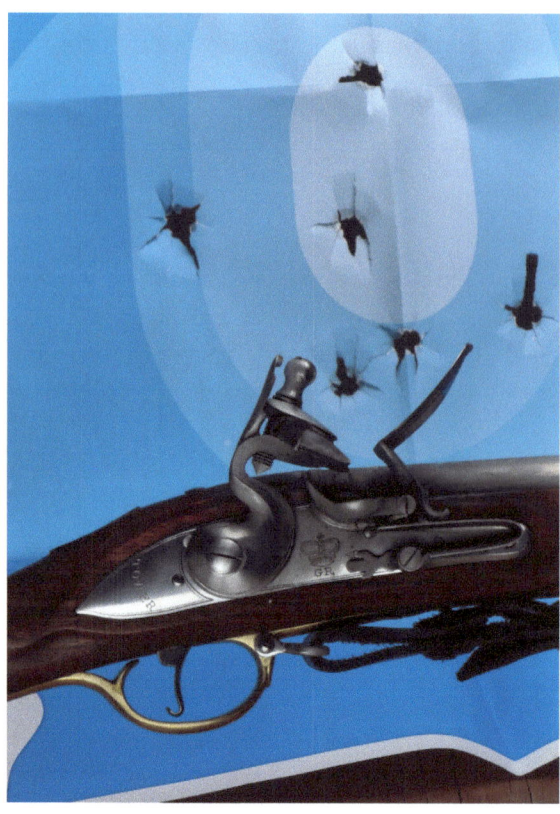

be an investment piece, while the repros will likely depreciate rather than appreciate to any degree. Repros look just as good on the wall, though.

And you can *shoot* repros. As many colonials found, smoothbore muskets made decent hunting arms when loaded with patched roundball. Shooting patched ball from mine gave pleasing 5-shot groups at 50-yard of 5 inches or so. The bayonet stud makes a decent aiming reference. Pedersoli's Brown Bess fits me pretty well, and allows me to align my eye consistently with the bayonet stud better than other smoothbore arms. As with a shotgun, your eye is the rear sight, and the gun's fit is crucial to pointing it consistently. I lucked into a pretty good patch/ball combination on the first try in the .75 caliber bore. Using a .735-inch ball and a .010-inch patch lubed with Lehigh Valley Patch Lube gave me best results. A .015-inch patch was too hard to load. The Lehigh Patch lube scrubbed the bore sufficiently between shots no cleaning had to be performed until final cleanup after 25 shots or so.

Having finished the chronograph work first, the paper cartridges were fired using a standing rest attached to the chronograph's tripod. Sometimes paper cartridges group a little better with a fouled barrel, so I was quite pleased to achieve a 5-shot group at 25 yards of 3 inches. The paper cartridges had a .715-inch ball over 100 grains of Swiss Fg. The group from the slightly fouled bore was far better than the Indian reproduction ever achieved. If the grouping held, that load would translate into 6 or 7 inches at 50 yards, and 12 or 14 at 100.

All in all, a good smoothbore musket can be a relaxing and rewarding range

Rifles, Rangers & Revolution

Paper cartridge accuracy is very good. The Pedersoli musket is very well made and consistent. Paper cartridges (left) delivered a 3-inch group at 25 yards from a standing rest in a slightly fouled bore. (Smoothbores often shoot a little better with paper cartridges in a lightly fouled barrel.) The moment of ignition shooting the Pedersoli Brown Bess (right). Its superior barrel delivers a fun and unique shooting experience!

experience. The ease of loading a patched ball compared to the rifle is a pleasure, and there is less fuss involved. The satisfying *thwap* a musket ball makes impacting the target backing is extremely rewarding. That I can shoot all day for pennies is another reason this musket is in my range rotation.

Clean up is best done with the barrel in the stock, since it is pinned into the wood, and driving them in and out will eventually cause loosening and may damage the wood. Plug the touch hole, pour in hot water with Dawn dish soap, plug the muzzle (your palm works if the water isn't too hot) and shake. Pour out, repeat. Ninety percent of your work is done. Follow up with patches and a good bore solvent like Birchwood Casey No. 77 (good patch lube, too) since it is relatively inexpensive. Some water will leak, so be sure and dry the wood thoroughly. I sometimes eschew hot water and just use No. 77. I've found Shooter's Choice FP-10 one of the best modern oils for lubrication and use as a preservative. It sticks to the metal, and I've never had after rust using FP-10. The Brown Bess, and all smoothbores, come to think of it, are fun at the range. I don't have to walk as far to change targets, and they are easier to load and shoot than a rifle.

Pistols were scarce commodities and both sides used whatever could be had. French, English and American made guns were bought, stolen or captured and pressed into service. Since the official British issue was the Eliott Light Dragoon, one was procured from Loyalist Arms in Canada. A bit pudgy on arrival, the judicious use of a rasp and polishing paper improved its looks dramatcially. There is a nice pistol lurking under the somewhat indifferent Indian workmanship.

Rifles, Rangers & Revolution

Chapter 33
The Eliott Light Dragoon Pistol

The Loyalist Arms import cleaned up nicely and shoots well.

THE COPY OF the Eliott Light Dragoon pistol imported by Loyalist Arms and Repairs in Nova Scotia isn't exactly like the ones pictured in DeWitt Bailey's *Small Arms of British Forces in North America* [3] or George C. Neumann's *Battle Weapons of the American Revolution*,[18] but it comes closer than the other imports available, and is less than half the cost of a Rifle Shoppe kit. Unboxing, it just looks a little bloated and rather ill.

A plus: Loyalist Arms checks lock function, hardens the frizzen to ensure it sparks, and drills the touchhole. Unfortunately, the bore is .60 caliber instead of the regulation .66 or something easy to get like .62. You also get to fire the "proof load" in the barrel (something best done from cover). Loyalist Arms provides instruction and means (except powder) to do so, which this barrel passed. I don't expect a long "service life," because it's a once a year fun gun for me. I'll get my money's worth. It's impressively large with a barrel length of 8½ inches and a hefty weight of 2 pounds, 11 ounces.

Few guns are as disappointing as these Indian-made replicas. All exhibit woeful craftsmanship or even feigned interest by the workmen, but there's a gem underneath. Since the Indians make models otherwise difficult or prohibitively expensive to acquire, I've remodeled three, and each one had slightly different (but not insurmountable) problems. Not for the faint of heart, almost every part needs some attention. As crude and indifferent as the fit and finish are, anyone who has built a gun kit will be able to transform one. At least all the holes are drilled, so you don't need machinery—just sweat and elbow grease.

Loyalist Arms stamped proofmarks on the barrel—the one part to treasure and save. Thankfully, the barrel was well polished and it trued up quickly without disturbing the proofs. The lockplate was a sadder story. It had "Tower 1760" cast in place in a modern font along with cast-in border engraving. The "Crown GR" was struck deep, and all the markings heavily buffed over and all square surfaces rounded.

The lockplate is soft, evidenced by the muscular workman striking the "Crown/GR" with such a heavy blow it bent the lockplate. Rather than

Friend Roger Renner takes a shot with the paper cartridges. Recoil is mild, and accuracy can be quite good. A fun pistol!

Paper cartridges at 10 yards grouped well (below left). That's three shots with two shots on the top right in the "7" zone. Tip: The gun was held so the red area and "X" of the target reflected in the top of the barrel at one spot. Removing excess wood slimmed the gun and hand polishing the brass smooths the uneven power polish (below, right). A nice touch, the barrel's proofmarks (bottom) were added by Loyalist Arms. Engraver Joe Scotton engraved "Tower" on the lockplate and added border engraving.

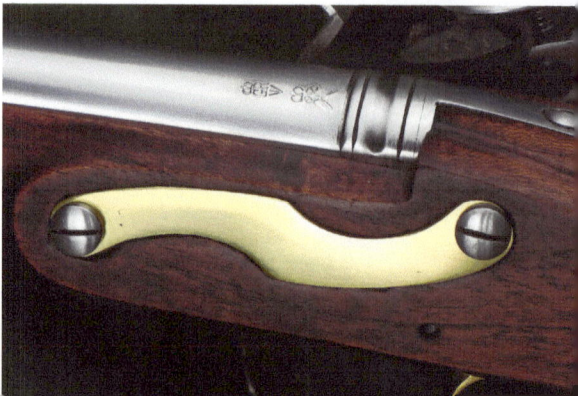

straighten it, they then ground the back flat so the mainspring would work. After striking the plate with a hammer to bend it back out a little, it filed easily and I did away with its cast-in markings.

Having been hardened, the frizzen required a stone to polish out, a little more arduous. After removing the plate markings, I had a choice. Leave them off as a "private purchase" pistol, or etch them back on and have new border lines engraved. Either way would look measurably better than the pistol had before. I chose both. Joe Scotton, who also engraved the Brown Bess lock, cut new borders on the hammer and plate. He touched up the newly etched "Tower" and "Crown GR" giving them the look of having been engraved.

Using over-the-counter Hornady .570 roundball got me shooting right away. Track of the Wolf's offers the recommended .580-inch roundball, and they were added for a second shooting session. Both were charged with 45 grains of Goex FFg instead of the recommended 30. Both loaded easily, recoiled lightly. Of the first ten cartridges, four were fired for fun, and six more reserved for groups in a fouled bore. All but one loaded easily with the pistol's rammer. After a ceasefire to change targets, round eight loaded hard enough to require a stouter pistol rod to fully seat the ball.

Aim Without Sights

What made this all worthwhile was a completely unexpected 2½-inch group at 10 yards. The first group was good enough I tried it again and achieved a 3-inch group. Secret: The group shown was made by holding the pistol down and aligning a reflection of the "X" in the red center of the target in the same place on the top of the polished barrel's surface. Looking *down* the barrel quadrupled the group size.

A little handwork turned an execrable piece of gun from sow's ear to silk purse (well, handsome *wool* purse anyway). Sans engraving, there is only your labor involved to complete the transformation. With engraving, the cost was still less than $700, and the gun looks great on display and is fun on the range.

Pistols were normally fired at contact range from horseback or simply point fired, so sights were never a consideration and neither was enjoying even modest accuracy. The sword was the primary weapon and the pistol for emergencies, since it was difficult to reload from horseback, and impossible to load during a meleé. Of all the weapons available in the day, and of all the weapons in this study, the pistol was the least important—until it was needed! Fired and flipped over, the butt with its solid brass cap makes an excellent skull cracker with the barrel as a handle giving great leverage. Simcoe's men were lucky if they had just one pistol, but a pair was standard issue.

Appendix i
Footnotes & Further Reading

[1] *Simcoe's Military Journal: A History of the Operations of a Partisan Corp, Called the Queen's Rangers, Commanded by Lieut. Col. J. G. Simcoe, During the War of the American Revolution; Now First Published with a Memoir of the Author and Other Additions*, A "Print on Demand" book from amazon.com.

[2] *British Military Flintlock Rifles: 1740-1840*, by DeWitt Bailey, ©2002, hardcover, 264 pages, 320 photos, 8.5x11, $47.95, ISBN: 1-931464-30-0, Mowbray Publishing, 54 East School Street, Woonsocket, RI 02895, (800) 999-4697, www.manatarmsbooks.com

[3] *Small Arms of the British Forces in America, 1664-1815*, by DeWitt Bailey, ©2009, hardcover, 368 pages, 400+ illustrations, 8.5x11, $59.99, ISBN: 1-931464-40-5, from Mowbray Publishing, 54 East School Street, Woonsocket, RI 02895, (800) 999-4697, www.manatarmsbooks.com

[4] *A History of the 3-Pound Verbruggen Gun and its Use in North America, 1775-1783*, Stephen G. Strach, 1986, Cowpens National Monument

[5] *History Of South Carolina 1775-1780*, by Edward McCrady, ©1901

[6] *The Public Papers of George Clinton, First Governor of New York*, 10 Vols., Albany, ©1900

[7] *Webster's Dictionary, 1828*, www.webstersdictionary1828.com

[8] *Ordnance Manual Use Officers United States Army 1850*, Scholarly Publishing Office, University of Michigan Library, ISBN: 978-1425559717

[9] *The Queen's Rangers, A pamphlet issued in connection with the presentation of the colors of the Queen's Rangers to the Public Library of Toronto*, by Frederick M. Robins of that city. OP, 1923, The Public Library of Toronto,)

[10] *The Black Hussars, A Brief and Concise History of Frederick Diemar's Hussars*, by Dr. Gary Corrado, ©2011, Heritage Books, 100 Railroad Ave, #104, Westminster, MD, 21157 ISBN: 978-0-7884-3540-9

[11] *Grasshoppers and Butterflies, the Light 3 Pounders of Pattison and Townsend*, by Adrian B. Caruana, ©1979, 1999, OP, ISBN: 0-919316-39-5, Museum Restoration Service, P.O. Box 70, Alexandria Bay, NY 13607, (613) 393-2980

(12) *The Brown Bess, An Identification and Illustrated Study of Britain's Most Famous Musket*, by Erik Goldstein and Stuart Mowbray, ©2010, $39.99, 10x8, 160 pages, 959 full color illustrations, Softcover, ISBN: 1-931464-44-8, Publisher: Mowbray Publishing, 54 East School Street, Woonsocket, RI 02895, (800) 999-4697, www.manatarmsbooks.com

(13) *The Administration of the Massachusetts and Virginia Navies of the American Revolution*, Charles Oscar Paullin, ©1906, via Internet Archive, www.archive.org.

(14) *Treatise on Partisan Warfare*, Johann von Ewald, translation, introduction, and annotation by Robert A Selig and David Curtis Skaggs, ©1991, ISBN 0-313-27350-2

(15) *Hand-Book for Hythe*, by Hans Busk, ©1860, reprinted 1971 by Richmond Publishing Co. Ltd., Richmond, Surrey, England

(16) *Eighteenth Century Gunfounding*, by Melvin H. Jackson and Charles de Beer, ©1974, OP, Smithsonian Institution Press, LCCCN 73-5882

(17) *Rethinking the Potter: The Truth Behind the Revolutionary War's ultimate Sword*, by Erik Goldstein, ©2007 Man At Arms for the Gun and Sword Collector, Vol. 29, No. 5, Mowbray Publishing, 54 East School Street, Woonsocket, RI 02895, (800) 999-4697, www.manatarmsbooks.com

(18) *Battle Weapons of the American Revolution* by George C. Neumann, ©2011, softcover, 8.5x11, 393 pages, 2200+ photos, ISBN 13: 9781931464499, from Mowbray Publishing, 54 East School Street, Woonsocket, RI 02895, (800) 999-4697, www.gunandswordcollector.com

Appendix ii
Notes About the Paintings

THE PORTRAIT OF John Graves Simcoe (Jean Laurent Mosnier, 1791), the Rifleman of the Queen's Rangers and Infantryman and Hussar of the Queen's Rangers (Capt. Murray circa 1780) are from the Toronto Public Library. Prints are available (see Appendix v). Murray's paintings were colored in the early 1900s, but were drawn from life.

Jan Verbruggen Foundry drawings courtesy Semeijns de Vries van Doesburgh Foundation www.janverbruggen.com. Some dispute the drawings were made by Jan Verbruggen, but he was an artist of considerable talent leaving behind a small body of paintings. They are quite well done, so it is hard to imagine the foundry drawings are the work of another, even if the foundry was running at full tilt. Another interesting point is the perspective is so good, there is speculation they were made using a camera obscura. The Foundry drawings were also part of the Verbruggen Inheritance and considered their private property, another good reason they are attributed to Jan.

While not positively identified, it is guessed the elderly gentleman looking on during the pouring of the metal just might be Jan Verbruggen. No other image of him is known to exist. Detail from Foundry Drawing 39, courtesy the van Doesburgh Foundation.

Appendix iii
Weights and Measures of the Arms

P1776 Muzzleloading Infantry Rifle

Maker:	The Rifle Shoppe, Inc. 870740 S. Hwy. 177 Wellston, OK 74881 (405) 356-2583 www.therifleshoppe.com
Action type:	Conventional flintlock muzzleloader
Caliber:	.62 (patched roundball)
Barrel length:	28 inches
Overall length:	44¾ inches
Weight:	8½ pounds
Finish:	Brown
Sights:	3-leaf rear, brass blade front
Stock:	English walnut, oil finish
Price:	$1,195 (Kit w/assembled lock for advanced builders)

.62 Caliber Muzzleloader Performance

Bullet	Powder	Charge	Velocity	Group Size
(bullet weight, type)	(brand)	(grains weight)	(fps)	(inches)
325 RB*	Goex FFFg	85	1,417	3¾
325 RB*	O. E. FFFg	85	1,464	3¼

Notes: *Track of the Wolf cast roundball. O.E. is Olde Eynsford. Groups the product of 3 shots at 100 yards. Chronograph screens set 10 feet from the muzzle. One Ox Yoke Wonder Wad placed over the powder and a 0.600-inch ball, 0.010-inch patch lubed with Lehigh Valley Patch Lube (used on all loads).

P1776 Ferguson

Maker:	The Rifle Shoppe
Action type:	Breechloading single-shot flintlock
Caliber:	.62 (0.615-inch roundball greased with 2:1 beeswax/tallow)
Barrel length:	33 inches
Overall length:	50 inches
Weight:	9 pounds, 9 ounces
Finish:	Brown
Sights:	Steel blade front, 2-leaf rear
Stock:	Walnut
Price:	$2,000 (Kit for advanced builders)

Ferguson Rifle Performance

Bullet	Powder	Charge	Velocity	Group Size
(bullet weight, type)	(brand)	(grains weight)	(fps)	(inches)
355 RB*	O.E. FFFg	50	1,101	3¼

Notes: Hand cast roundball from Jeff Tanner mold, dipped in a 50/50 mix of mutton tallow and beeswax. O.E. is Olde Eynsford. Groups the product of 3 shots at 100 yards. Chronograph screens set 10 feet from muzzle. No wiping occurred during this shooting. Breech screw cleaned as necessary.

Brown Bess

Maker:	**Davide Pedersoli** Via Artigiani, 57 25063 Gardone Val Trompia Brescia, Italy www.davide-pedersoli.com
Importer:	**Dixie Gun Works** P.O. Box 130 1412 West Reelfoot Ave. Union City, TN 38282 (731) 885-0561, www.dixiegunworks.com
Action type:	Smoothbore flintlock musket
Caliber:	.75
Barrel length:	41¼ inches
Overall length:	58½ inches
Weight:	9 pounds
Finish:	Polished steel
Sights:	None, bayonet stud serves as reference
Stock:	European walnut
Price:	$1,395

.75 Caliber Smoothbore Performance

Bullet (bullet weight, type)	Powder (brand)	Charge (grains weight)	Velocity (fps)	Group Size (inches)
557 RB*	Swiss Fg**	100	897	3
594 RB*	O. E. FFg***	80	1,098	5¼

Notes: *Track of the Wolf brand Roundball. O.E. is Olde Eynsford. Chronograph screens set 10 feet from muzzle. **Paper cartridge with .715 RB; Group the product of 5 shots at 25 yards. ***Track of the Wolf .735 RB patched with 0.010-inch Ox Yoke lubed with Lehigh Valley Patch Lube; Group the product of 5 shots at 50 yards.

Eliott Light Dragoon Pistol

Importer:	Loyalist Arms & Repairs 10 Brunt Road, Harrietsfield Nova Scotia, Canada B3V 1B1 (902) 479-0967 www.loyalistarms.ca
Action type:	Smoothbore flintlock pistol
Caliber:	.60
Barrel length:	8½ inches
Overall length:	15⅞ inches
Weight:	2 pounds, 11 ounces
Finish:	Polished steel
Sights:	None
Stock:	Walnut
Price:	$400

James Potter Light Dragoon Saber

Importer:	At The Royal Sword 2538 Rue Cuvillier, Montréal Québec, Canada H1W 3B1 (514) 522-3108, www.theroyalsword.com
Blade:	Carbon steel, 32½ inches long; 1⁷⁄₁₆ inches wide at the tang, tapering to 1³⁄₁₆ near the tip, sharpened along the length with a false edge at the tip of about 7 inches. No fuller.
Hilt:	6½ inches long, wood grip, wrapped in leather, bound in wire with iron guard.
Weight:	2 pounds, 9.2 ounces; 3 pounds, 1.7 ounces (sheathed)
Overall length:	39⅛ inches
Sheath:	Leather, wood lined with steel throat, frog button and chape.
Finish:	Natural, polished steel
Price:	$185

Notes: This Indian-made reproduction appears to be scaled to about 90 to 95% of the original. The iron guard is thinner, handle and blade shorter. The power polish leaves ripples in the blade, and the blade is without the false edge on top. Many of these features keep the cost of manufacturing down, ensure fakes can be spotted by collectors, all without affecting the reenactor's impression of the soldier to any great degree. The blade files easily (as I found adding the false edge), so it is not tempered.

3-Pounder Pattison "Grasshopper"

Cannon Tube:	**South Bend Replicas** 25639 Layton Rd. North Liberty, IN 46554 (574) 514-7571 www.southbendreplicas.com
Carriage:	Oak with iron trim (maker: Cannon Ltd., to British Ordnance Blueprints in 2004)
Caliber:	2¼ inch (1 pounder)
Barrel length:	3 feet, cast iron, steel lined
Overall length:	7½ feet
Width:	4½ feet
Height:	3½ feet
Weight:	Approx. 800 pounds including barrel; barrel about 200 pounds
Finish:	Gray and black paint
Sights:	None
Value:	$8,000 to $12,000

Notes: Almost all "3-pounder" guns made today have 2¼ inch bores. This allows the use of 2.02-inch iron roundshot—much easier to acquire than 2.77 inch of the regulation 3-pounder size, but it does make the gun a "1.1 pounder" truth be told, since that is what the balls weigh. The barrel is cast of iron rather than bronze, too, since bronze is still about six times the cost of iron. Bronze tubes are still firmly the province of Kings! Sadly, the carriage maker is no longer in business.

Appendix iv
Another Revolution Started with a Bang!

The little Grasshopper, the first gun cast at the rehabilitated Woolwich Arsenal, also set off the Industrial Revolution.

WHILE RESEARCHING a simple story about use of the 3-pounder Grasshopper cannon by the Queen's Rangers during the American Revolution, I discovered several unrelated anomalies. What follows outlines the bare bones of a course of research I plan to pursue in the years to come.

A puzzle kept bubbling up around the achievements of Jan Verbruggen's successful modernization of Woolwich Arsenal and the birth of the Industrial Revolution when iron magnate John Wilkinson brought James Watt's steam engine to fruition. Most histories recount these events as two distinctly separate occurrences, each happening as if in a vacuum. This I find hard to believe. Few scientific achievements occur in a vacuum, but the way and how cannon manufacturing was modernized began earlier than supposed in England rather than Switzerland, and all of it led to the Industrial Revolution's rise in England. Seems there was a lot more to the story.

Following the Trail

Trying to find the bread crumb trail between Verbruggen and Wilkinson lead to a longer one, one possibly only alive in my imagination since almost all evidence has been well scattered, and the trail cold in many spots. There is no concrete connection between Verbruggen and Wilkinson either, but I believe there is enough circumstantial evidence to connect them. I believe the even longer trail, however thin, connects cannon tube construction beginning with Prince Rupert, 1st Duke of Cumberland in the 1670s, then to Jean Maritz and Jan Verbruggen leading directly to the steam engine.

But first, the cannon and the Industrial Revolution, since that trail has the most credible evidence, however circumstantial. The part about Prince Rupert a full century earlier is mostly hunch, which is why it follows last.

This large mortar mold is made vertically rather than on a horizontal spindle as were cannon tubes. To the right of the mold between the vertical beams is the "strickle board" used to give this mortar its external shape. A small fire underneath gradually dries the mold while workmen add the trunnions and other decorations. Courtesy the van Doesburgh Foundation.

Most histories mention John "Iron Mad" Wilkinson as the man making the Industrial Revolution possible, but I believe credit should be shared with Jan Verbruggen of Woolwich Arsenal, and Member of Parliament Anthony Bacon, with an assist from the Royal Navy, the Board of Ordnance and Prince Rupert. While I've discovered no concrete connection between Verbruggen and Wilkinson, Bacon and Wilkerson were involved in the principal technology of iron mining (Bacon) and the foundry business (Wilkinson). Verbruggen specialized in bronze founding and is responsible for modernizing cannon manufacturing in England. Jan Verbruggen was up and running first. While few communications between these three has surfaced, it's hard to believe they didn't communicate at all.

The Trail Gets Warmer

Fact: Jan and Pieter Verbruggen move to Woolwich Arsenal in 1770, bringing along the new method of boring bronze cannon horizontally from solid castings against a fixed bit. (Most histories credit Jean Maritz of Switzerland for the method Verbruggen brings, and it is already in use in much of the world.) The modernization proposed by Verbruggen is considerable, since the arsenal was completely run down and barely operating.

It so happens, during the same year of 1770, the Royal Navy's iron cannon begin exploding in practice at an alarming rate. After an investigation, the prime contractor's cannon are found to be the ones failing, and existing ones given more extensive proofs also fail. The tubes in stores are held from issue, and tubes on ships recalled, leading to a reevaluation of iron cannon manufacturing (and a Naval crisis!). In June 1773, Jan Verbruggen is called on by the Board of Ordnance to assay some of the burst iron cannon, even though his specialty is bronze, something he freely admits. I believe it is probable Verbruggen consulted with iron masters, and John Wilkinson was one of the largest and most able.

In July 1773, the King visits the revitalized Woolwich arsenal to see the new machinery completed, and given a demonstration of how the process works, but Woolwich won't start operations for another month or two.

Anthony Bacon enters the story at the time the King is inspecting Woolwich. As a Member of Parliament, and a man in the iron mining business, Anthony Bacon is very likely aware early on of both the Royal Navy's problem, and of the modernization methods the Verbruggens are bringing to Woolwich. Bacon, who runs an iron and coal operation in Wales—but not a foundry—presents the Board of Ordnance with an offer to found three 18-pounder guns with his iron using different methods of smelting the iron, but cast around a newel bar forming the bore in the usual manner. This method casts the cannon tube with the bore formed by a bar, and is held vertically while a drill bit is rotated in to give a smooth finish to the rough cast bore. (3)

After submitting the three conventionally made tubes, Bacon then presents the Board with a fourth 18-pounder tube, cast solid and bored, and claims it was done at greater cost. All four of these tubes are manufactured by John Wilkinson. All tubes submitted by Bacon to the Board of Ordnance pass proofs at Woolwich, but the one bored from solid passes even excessive proof.

My guess: Bacon, who the has mines but no foundry, had interested Wilkinson in the process by dangling contracts for iron cannon, something the Royal Navy currently needed in abundance. Wilkinson invests in the horizontal boring engine while completing the conventionally cast and vertically drilled iron barrels, and has the system operating within a year.

Wandering Eye

I suspect Bacon has used his position as an MP, and his connections with the Board of Ordnance to study the methods the Verbruggens developed and disseminates the process to John Wilkinson, one of the few industrialists who is able to invest the money to duplicate the process for use on iron. This very likely does not involve any subterfuge. Even if Bacon didn't provide the plans for the machinery, I believe it's possible either someone at the Board of Ordnance, the Verbruggens or both would be forthcoming with advice and maybe even plans for the horizontal boring engine, since this was a matter of vital national interest.

This giant apparatus able to revolve castings weighing as much as four tons against a fixed bit had to be very expensive to build compared to the conventional method of holding the barrel upright and running in a bit to clean out the pre-cast bore. It is possible other plans were available for the process, but the closest ones visibly working were at Woolwich, and possibly copies of the plans available at the Board of Ordnance, since they held the purse strings and approved all of Verbruggen's modernization plans before paying for them.

Fast Work

The Verbruggens rebuilt Woolwich's furnace and built the boring engine in just a couple of years. The modernization includes a new process the Verbruggens add of outside turning of the entire tube. Some of these new tubes lack cast-in coats of arms or other decorations usually added to guns. Outside turning helps show the tubes have no flaws, and something cast-in flourishes would impede. This method will soon be adopted worldwide. Perhaps due to the exigency of war, it was decided not to add any unnecessary embellishments to the tubes. None of the 3-pounder tubes have any.

I believe it possible Verbruggen saw or heard about Prince Rupert's "nealed and turned" Patent guns made in the late 1600s (see page 163), since some survive to this day, and they were marvels when they were made. I'd be surprised if Verbruggen wasn't given a tour of the Tower of London. It's not hard to believe one of the men employed there would be well educated on the subjects in his care, and enthusiastically show Jan one of Rupert's guns while explaining the benefits of the Prince's processes (although his process was a mystery by the late 1700s. Prince Rupert's patents are too obscure for anyone to duplicate his process. If enthusiasts back then were like they are today, they were probably quite knowledgeable on the history of English cannon founding. Neither Maritz nor Verbruggen were known for outside turning of the tubes prior to Verbruggen's arrival at Woolwich as far as I can find.

Extra! Read All About It!

Verbruggen's new guns are well thought of. Newspaper accounts extol their virtue saying, "The brass guns, consisting of twelve and six pounders, cast by the famous Messrs. John and Peter Verbruggen, made a most elegant appearance, not only by the curious workmanship, but by their judicious choice and scientific mixture of several kinds of metal, who have undoubtedly cast, and are casting such a train of artillery, as the oldest and most experienced Officers confess never to have seen before. They were so highly polished, both within and without, that every beholder viewed them with astonishment. They were so exceedingly beautiful, that the Gunners were even afraid to handle them. They not only stood the usual proof, but were afterwards found to be so completely perfect in every respect, that his Lordship expressed his utmost satisfaction." [4]

For Wilkinson to have a similar operation in place, capable of delivering a tube in 1773, I believe he would needed the design in hand for the machinery. He was already a master founder. It is noted that, "Practically nothing is known about Bacon's operation and it is doubtful if he was operating a foundry of his own. He was either associated with or was acting on behalf of John Wilkinson who at this time had in operation his iron-boring mill that was patented on 27 January 1774. Wilkinson's boring mill, if one can judge from the patent sketch, was essentially the same tool as the Verbruggens' which at the time already stood installed at the foundry." [1]

Time and Money

Even with the plans helping him shave the precious time it would take to build the machinery, I don't believe Wilkinson would have invested in this process until he discovered it hadn't been patented, and saw a patent as a way to lock out competition and allow him to recoup his investment in the machinery more quickly. Bacon then contracts to provide 300 tons of ordnance at same rate as hollow-cast guns, since the Board of Ordnance is adamant about controlling costs and refuses to pay extra for their more complicated manufacture. Another major consideration Wilkinson would face was the fact the amount of iron bored from the tubes was scrap good only for cannon balls, whereas bronze could go right back into the pot. Refused the extra costs endured using the new process, Wilkinson would have to make it up elsewhere.

All these considerations were important since the first argument between Bacon and the Board of Ordnance is over the increased cost of casting the barrels solid and boring them. While Bacon asks for £20 per ton, the Board demands they cost the £18 p/ton currently paid for tubes cast around a newel bar. A patent is looking more important to the investment, since not a penny more is going to be forthcoming from the government. The material removed is considerable, so it is measurable extra cost in addition to the extra time required to drill the bore from solid.

As for the patent, gunfounding was the province of kings worldwide, and no king or crown armory would need a patent. But the technique the Verbruggens used was new in England. With no existing patent, Wilkinson, applied for and received one. Wilkinson knew competition would make it harder to recoup his tooling costs, since he would share the volume of orders with other foundries, eliminating any negotiating leverage for a higher price. He was prescient.

Passed!

Impressed at the way Wilkinson's tube passes proof, the Board orders all iron cannon made this way by the several private enterprises supplying the Navy. Wilkinson is the only one able to do this because of his patent, and this gives him the head start he needs. The Board of Ordnance is surprised and alarmed to find the process patented. The book E*ighteenth Century Gunfounding* notes the Crown declared the Verbruggen process secret, a strange thing to say about a process already in use worldwide. [1] If it's true the process was declared secret, perhaps that is why the patent examiners could find no evidence to deny Wilkinson's claim. The Crown wouldn't need a patent anyway.

The Board probably thought Wilkinson had a lot of cheek patenting the process. More so if (as I suspect) they had helped him with plans for the machinery! Wilkinson's patent was eventually cancelled in the "national interest" but he had time to recoup some tooling costs, and a head start since his operation was up and running, while others would have to build the apparatus. In 1776, Bacon reports to the Board his agreement with John Wilkinson is ended and he has made arrangements to provide cannon bored from solid at £18 per ton. [3] So now we know the cat is out of the bag.

I suspect Wilkinson has been looking for other ways to make his expensive machinery investment pay, especially since the patent is in the process of being overturned almost before the ink dries. Watt's steam cylinders are a natural, and likely easily adapted to Wilkinson's new machinery. Watt had been struggling over how do this for several years, and his engine can't reach its full potential using iron plate wrapped into a cylinder, although the method works for the more primitive Newcomen Engine long in service across England.

The Industrial Revolution Begins

It's possible Wilkinson, as one of the biggest iron producers, had been approached by Watt with the idea of making steam cylinders before, but couldn't see enough business to warrant building the new, expensive machinery, especially since someone has to make a steam engine cylinder before Watt can prove its benefit. After all, it was only a theory that the steam engine will be a vast improvement over the waterwheel and Newcomen engines. Their principles are well understood.

If Watt's engine works, great, but it will take time to sell them to people already invested in time-proven methods. Watt realized his "fire-engine" can never reach its full potential the way he's currently making them. In 1875, Watt works to have his patent extended, while his partner Boulton experiments on their Soho engine. Samuel Smiles [5] notes, "A new 18-inch cylinder had been cast for it at Bersham by John Wilkinson, the great iron founder, who contrived a machine for boring it with accuracy." Unmentioned is Wilkinson's patent is still in force, and Watt has no choice but to go to Wilkinson for a cylinder bored from solid.

It takes time and salesmanship before the steam engine replaces both waterwheels and Newcomen engines, but many Newcomens have been at work so long they're in need of repair or replacement. Water, of course, is dependent on a river and some waterworks lie unused for months during low water. Smiles notes, "Wilkinson's iron-manufacturing neighbors, who were contemplating the erection of Newcomen engines, suspended their operations until they had the opportunity to see what the Boulton and Watt's engine could do." Far more efficient than a Newcomen engine, Watt's steam engine uses far less fuel—its chief selling point.

Wilkinson installs his first new steam engine to pump water back up to the waterwheel that powered his foundry's bellows. His engine begins operating in 1776. With the boring method locked up in a patent, Wilkinson is the only one able to make steam engine cylinders, too. Wilkinson had the head start he needed, and Boulton and Watt placed orders for more cylinders. This leads me to believe the genesis of Wilkinson's ability to create steam cylinders "bored to truth" begins with the cannon.

I've found little evidence to support my theories other than placing the men close enough together in time and circumstance and inference from the surviving documents. Most histories credit Wilkinson for starting the Industrial Revolution, but it is hard for me to believe Wilkinson came up with the ideas and invested in the tooling to machine the massive iron castings for a steam engine in a vacuum separate from the signal advancements of the Verbruggens and modernization of Woolwich Arsenal. And I seriously doubt he would make the investment without the steady income cannon tubes would generate.

History has ignored the contributions of the Verbruggens to the Industrial Revolution. It is understandable if you think of Jan and Pieter as men leading satisfying lives as Crown employees. Living in a fine house built for them on the Arsenal, their chief headache was getting their bills paid in a timely fashion, and they were likely the last people who would have seen the need or tried to exploit their contributions outside of their employment. Besides, there was a war on, and they had their hands full.

The Verbruggens didn't need to promote ideas and protect intellectual works to remain successful. Jan quietly passed from history (except among artillerists), and Pieter followed him quickly soon after the conclusion of hostilities, leaving them no time to create memoirs. Wilkinson and Watt never tired of telling people about their achievements and got the glory—glory likely impossible to attain without the signal advancements in the manufacturing of the cannon. That's not a cynical assessment. As men living on their wits, their continued success required self-promotion and continual new ideas to create and sustain business, unlike a Crown employee.

Prince Rupert's Patent Guns

Our little breadcrumb trail vanishes for long stretches as we go back in time to the late 1600s, and the following has little supporting evidence beyond my imagination (at least yet). I believe the thread connecting cannons to the Industrial Revolution goes 100 years more into the past. The general timeline begins in the 1670s when Prince Rupert, 1st Duke of Cumberland, turns his gentlemanly eye to science. His experiments in iron cannon founding lead to his manufacturing "patent 'nealed and turned guns" costing three times as much as "rough guns," yet half the cost of bronze ones.

Prince Rupert casts his guns either solid or with a core (this part is a little fuzzy), anneals them in a fashion not recorded to make them as malleable as wrought iron, (how is not completely understood even today), and bores them to caliber while turning them smooth outside. Contemporary accounts praise their finish inside and out. (2) They also shoot truer, which makes me think he cast them solid. At this time, most cannon were bored out by running a turning bit into the tube as it was held vertically. I suspect Prince Rupert laid the cannon on their side to perform the boring and lathe turning of the outside. It is the only practical way to do both. Using a fixed bit, and then turning the annealed tube would make it easier to bore the tubes concentric whether cast solid or with a core, while turning the outside.

After this method is proven, a group of men take their incomplete understanding of Prince Rupert's process (and without much knowledge of iron, either) to France, where they fail to successfully duplicate his method, but disseminate the idea of casting guns and boring them true, which was highly problematic for the French. As an aside, this episode would've made a superb 1950s Alec Guinness/Peter Sellers comedy, since the cannons are spectacular failures and the principals succumb to intriguing against one another. One claim was to produce a "mortar to be spotted like a Leopard with white and red spotts only out of Iron." Of course they failed, raising suspicion among the French. (2)

Whatever benefits Rupert's system brings is lost on the French due to the failure of the Englishmen and their lack of understanding of the principals of iron or even iron founding itself. Nonetheless, in *Prince Rupert's Patent Guns*, Sarah Bailey reports one of the Englishmen produced a book with drawings to explain how cannon were cast, bored and turned because his French was terrible.

Connections

We now have the process a lot closer to Jean Maritz, and described with pictures in a book. About the time Maritz is born, England weighs the cost vs. benefit of Prince Rupert's patent guns and determines they aren't worth the extra expense. That pretty much ends their purchase. The family that took over the business from Prince Rupert goes out of business and disappears along with the methods employed in annealing the guns. England returns to making guns the old way, casting the tube around a core so the bore is mostly formed. Prince Rupert's patent remains, but it is so obscure, little can be gleaned about the way he made his tubes.

My guess: The cannon casting community was very small, and it wouldn't surprise me anecdotal accounts of Rupert's process reached Maritz, albeit 20 years later, and he possibly saw the book of drawings eventually. Rupert sold his tubes to other countries as well as England, so their reputation is not just localized. Even if the story of the Englishmen coming to France and making fools of themselves had been presented as a funny story, good engineer that he was, it wouldn't take Maritz long to see the benefits of the horizontal process. In his original process, Maritz lowered the tube vertically onto a rotating bit. It was not a good system.

The lost alchemy around iron Rupert used could be discarded using bronze, and the concept of boring the gun horizontally solved myriad problems whether iron or bronze. Maritz possibly came up with the concept of the horizontal bed himself, but he began casting tubes solid and boring them horizontally. If the book of drawings showing Rupert's process exists (or even a record of it having existed), it would help link Rupert to Maritz. Once perfected, the Maritz system is adopted by others (including Holland), but not the English.

That England had to hire a Dutchman to bring the process back home to England is ironic. But I believe the concept now came full circle with John Wilkinson using the Verbruggen's manufacturing process on iron—an element now better understood than in Prince Rupert's days. The voodoo of annealing is supplanted by better understanding of the iron founding process, and better, higher quality steel cutters.

And there's the tiny bread crumb trail stopping and starting as it meanders across England, France, Switzerland and Holland over the 100 years between Prince Rupert and James Watts' steam engine.

I believe they are all connected.

Further Reading

[1] *Eighteenth Century Gunfounding*, by Melvin H. Jackson and Charles de Beer, ©1974, Smithsonian Institution Press, LCCCN 73-5882

[2] *Prince Rupert's Patent Guns*, by Sarah Barter Bailey, ©2000 The Trustees of the Armouries, Royal Armouries Museum, Armouries Drive, Leeds LS10 1LT, ISBN: 0948092297

[3] *Industrial South Wales 1750-1914*, Essays in Welsh Economic History, Edited by W.E. Minchinton, ©1969 Frank Cass & Co. Ltd, ISBN 714613444

[4] *Leeds Intelligencer,* Tuesday, April 26, 1774, ©British Library Board

[5] *Our Coal and Iron Industries, and the Men Who Have Wrought in Connection With Them*, by John Randall, F.G.S., ©1917, Barro-In-Furness, Reprinted by the Barrow News & Mail, Ltd.

Appendix v
Sutlers Row

Below are all the people I purchased goods from for the photos and the shooting. Many of my orders were minuscule and included only one or two items. All treated me as well as if I was spending hundreds. They are all very nice and easy to deal with and deserve your business.

Avalon Forge, 409 Gun Road, Baltimore, MD 21227, (410) 242-8431, www.avalonforge.com

Beeswax Candle Works, P.O. Box 1450, Cottage Grove, OR, 97424, (541) 942-7061, www.beeswaxcandleworks.com

Brownells, 200 South Front St., Montezuma, IA 50171, (800) 741-0015, www.brownells.com

Buffalo Arms, 660 Vermeer Ct., Ponderay, ID 83852, (208) 263-6953, www.buffaloarms.com

C & D Jarnagin, 113 North Fillmore St., Corinth, MS 38834, (662) 287-4977, www.jarnaginco.com

Crazy Crow, P.O. Box 847, Pottsboro, TX 75076, (903)786-2287, www.crazycrow.com

Dixie Gun Works, P.O. Box 130, 1412 West Reelfoot Ave., Union City, TN 38282, (731) 885-0561, www.dixiegunworks.com

G. Gedney Godwin, P.O. Box 100, Valley Forge, PA 19481, (610) 783 0670, www.gggodwin.com

Goex, Old Eynsford, Hodgdon Powder, 6430 Vista Dr., Shawnee, KS 66218, (913) 362-9455, www.goexpowder.com

The Gun Works Muzzleloading Emporium, 247 South 2nd St., Springfield, OR 97477, (541) 741-4118, www.thegunworks.com

Hobbylinc, 10101 Davis St., STE 600, Braselton, GA 30517, (888) 327-9673, www.hobbylinc.com

Hornady, P.O. Box 1848, Grand Island, NE 68802, (308) 382-1390, www.hornady.com

Hot Dip Tin, (801) 360-0707, www.hotdiptin.com

Hussar Saddlery, 853 Brunstetter Rd., Warren, OH 44481, (330) 360-8640, www.hussarsaddlery.com

Lehigh Valley Patch Lube, 474 West 3rd Street South, Fulton, NY 13069, www.lehighvalleylube.com

Jim Keller Historical Reenactment, www.jgkeller.ca

Martronics Corp., Etch-O-Matic, P.O. Box 200, Salkum, WA 98582, (360) 985-2999, www.etch-o-matic.com

McMaster-Carr, P.O. Box 54960, Los Angeles, CA 90054, (562) 692-5911, www.mcmaster.com

Powderhorns & More, Gerry Messmer, Owner, 410 Church St., Odessa, NY 14869, (910) 964-2580, www.powderhornsandmore.com

The Rifle Shoppe, 870740 S Hwy 177, Wellston, OK 74881, (405) 356-2583, www.therifleshoppe.com

Royal Artillery Museum, Building 402, Wilson Road, Larkhill, Salisbury, SP4 8QT, www.royalartillerymuseum.com

Joe Scotton Engraving, (310) 227-1341

Smiling Fox Forge, 3500 C.R. 234, Fremont, OH 43420, (419) 334-8180, www.smilingfoxforge.com (tow waste, patch worms)

Clay Smith Guns, 4560 Village Park Dr. East, Williamsburg, VA 23185, 757-871-9424, www.claysmithguns.com

Speer, 2299 Snake River Avenue, Lewiston, ID 83501, (800) 379-1732, www.speer-bullets.com

Steel Supply, 14130 West Rd., Houston, TX 77041, (713) 991-7600, www.steelsupplylp.com

Swiss, Wano Powder, Schuetzen Powder, 7650 US Hwy. 287, #100, Arlington, Texas 76001, (66) 809-9704, www.schuetzenpowder.com

Jeff Tanner Molds, 23 Passingham Avenue, South Green, Billericay, Essex, England, CM11 2TD, www.ballmoulds.com

Jas. Townsends, P.O. Box 415, Pierceton, IN 46562, (800) 338-1665, www.townsends.us

Track of the Wolf, 18308 Joplin St. N.W., Elk River, MN 55330, (763) 633-2500, www.trackofthewolf.com

Toronto Public Library, (416) 397-5981, www.torontopubliclibrary.ca

Trail Rock Ordnance, 1754 Little Valley Rd., Blaine, TN 37709, (865) 932-1200, www.trailrockordnance.com

Triton Works Custom Scabbards, www.tritonworks.com

White Dragon Paper, www.whitedragonpaper.com

About the Author

Jeff John, publisher of Art In Arms Press, is the former editor of *GUNS Magazine*, was an Associate Editor for Petersen's *Guns & Ammo* and Technical Editor for *Handguns* and *RifleShooter* magazines. He has had a lifelong interest in history, firearms, target shooting, gun making and photography.

In Print Now!

The Art in Arms Book No. 1
FG42

WWII Germany's innovative FG42 took the primary infantry rifle from a slow-firing pre-1900 bolt-action rifle to an ultra-fast machine rifle. *FG42* includes an in-depth review of the SMG Guns semi-auto replica. Includes shooting tips, fieldstripping, handloading tips and resource guide.

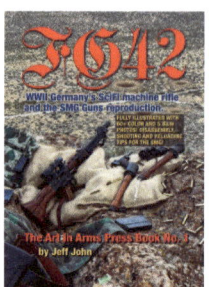

The Art In Arms Book No. 2
The Matchless Enfield No. 4 Mk I (T) Sniper

Britain created World War II's most effective sniper rifle starting with the war's best bolt-action battle rifle. *The Matchless Enfield* tells the story of the elite marksmen who used the No. 4 Mk I (T) sniper with skill and cunning dominating the battlefield. The No. 4 (T)'s on-range performance is evaluated by shooting an original. Included is an evaluation of the specialized gear including the unique 20X telescope, binocular, transit chest and other gear the sniper teams used on their stalks into the enemy's lines. Includes shooting tips, handloading and resource guide.

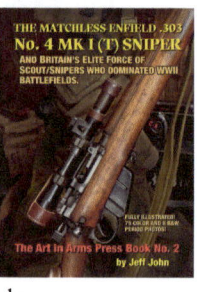

Coming Soon!
FG42 2nd Edition

The newly revised *FG42 2nd Edition* features all new chapters about the early Type I FG42 using the new reproduction from SMG Guns. The evolution of the FG42 in its scant few years of production are explored including full shooting tests of both reproductions.

The Art in Arms Book No. 4
The Smallbore Whitney Kennedy Lever Action Rifles

Winchester's only early competition was the unique Whitney rifle action pioneered by Andrew Burgess, an arms designer rivaling John Moses Browning in patented designs. The smallbore rifles in .44-40 with "S" lever and Loop lever are presented along with the very rare Whitney Scharf lever action.

The Art in Arms Book No. 5
The .303-inch BREN Gun

Top banana among Light Machine Guns, this Czech-designed LMG served Britain superlatively for more than six decades.

www.ingramcontent.com/pod-product-compliance
Lightning Source LLC
Chambersburg PA
CBHW041544220426
43665CB00002B/27